ISBN 978-1-331-34369-1
PIBN 10177015

1 MONTH OF
FREE
READING

at

www.ForgottenBooks.com

By purchasing this book you are eligible for one month membership to ForgottenBooks.com, giving you unlimited access to our entire collection of over 1,000,000 titles via our web site and mobile apps.

To claim your free month visit:

www.forgottenbooks.com/free177015

STUDIES OF THE PORTRAIT
OF CHRIST

STUDIES OF THE PORTRAIT OF CHRIS

BY THE REV. GEORGE MATHESON

M.A., D.D., F.R.S.E., FORMERLY MINISTER

OF THE PARISH OF ST. BERNARD'S

EDINBURGH

VOLUME II

LONDON

HODDER AND STOUGHTON

27 PATERNOSTER ROW

1900

Edinburgh : T. and A. Constable, Printers to Her Majesty

PREFACE TO VOLUME I

IN these pages I have endeavoured to trace the spiritual development, not of the life, but of the work, of Jesus exhibited in the Gospel narrative. Necessarily, therefore, I have fixed my attention not on the Divine or miraculous, but on the human, side of Christ. There can be no development in *miracles*; it is as wonderful to be an *inch* above nature as to be a mile. Being a study of development, the chapters, though very short, are rigidly connected and cannot be read in isolation. The book is not an abstract essay with foot-notes and references; it is semi-devotional; each chapter ends either with an invocation or a prayer. Having completed the first part of the studies I offer it by way of instalment and by way of experiment. Should it meet with general sympathy I should like to pursue the narrative to its close.

G. M.

EDINBURGH, 1899.

a 2

PREFACE

I HERE resume the Narrative from the point at which my first volume closed—the feeding of the multitude in the desert of Bethsaida. To every word of the previous Preface I adhere; I add a few remarks by way of elucidation. By the Title of this Book I do not mean a study of the different Portraits which have been drawn of Christ, nor even a comparison of the Pictures drawn by the Four Evangelists. The Portrait of Christ is to me the united impression produced upon the heart by these four delineations. My office is not that of a critic, not that of a creator, not that of an amender, but simply that of an interpreter; I study the Picture as it is.

I am glad that the reception by the public has invited me to pursue the subject. I am specially glad that I have not been suspected of a wish to minimise the Divine side of

Christianity. I have been for years persuaded, and with an ever-increasing conviction, that there is an element in Christ which is not to be explained by the stream of human heredity, but which implies an original Divine Sonship. But there is also confessedly that which *was* human—that which hungered, thirsted, hoped, feared, grew. I believe it grew into a progressive recognition of the steps of that redeeming work for the sake of which He was born, and which was already completed in the heart of the Father—that work whose every step was an act in that great Death-Sacrifice which reached from the depths of the Wilderness to the heights of Calvary. The light which is a unity in the sky is given in fragments by the pool; even so on the waters of earth was the *plan of the Father* revealed in fragments. The aim of this book is to *piece* these fragments. I have alluded only to those incidents which bear on the development. For this reason I have paused at Calvary, which is professedly the development's close.

G. M.

EDINBURGH, 1900.

CONTENTS

CHAPTER I

CHAPTER II

CHAPTER III

CHAPTER IV

CHAPTER V

CHAPTER VI

CONTENTS

CHAPTER XIV

CHAPTER XV

CHAPTER XVI

CHAPTER XVII

CHAPTER XVIII

CHAPTER XIX

CHAPTER XX

CONTENTS

CHAPTER I

THE FADING OF CHRIST'S FIRST HOPE

THE last glimpse we had of the Portrait of Jesus was in a light beginning to be overcast. He had crossed a transition line. In the very blaze of His fame He had met with His first real disappointment. I say 'disappointment,' not 'reverse.' The crowd had not deserted *Him*; *He* had fled from the crowd. He had found that He and they were seeking different things. His solitude was as yet only inward. The multitude were still on His side, but He felt that they were on His side by reason of a delusion. He perceived that He and they were using the phrase 'kingdom of God' in a different sense, in an opposite sense. To them it meant purple, fine linen, faring sumptuously every day; to Him it was an influence from within, which would make even vile raiment beautiful.

I have already said that in my opinion the earliest hope of Jesus was that during His life on earth He might witness the establishment of a kingdom of righteousness; this hope I have called His first ideal. I have also expressed my view of the *nature* of this kingdom which glittered in the soul of Jesus. I should not call it an inward kingdom. It was rather a kingdom *from* within. It did contemplate an influence on the surface, or, rather, a series of influences in which different men were to exert on society different degrees of power. But then, these degrees of power were to be proportionate to the sacrificial spirit. The influence was not to interfere from the *outside.* The kingdom of Jesus demanded no smashing up of the Roman Empire, no drastic upheaval of existing orders. It was to be something which could enter the present dwelling without breaking the doors. It was to come silently, unobtrusively. It was to demand no extra space; it was to work, like the leaven, through existing spaces. Its entrance was to abolish nothing; it was to act by addition, not by subtraction. It was to add to the world as it then stood this new commandment, 'Love one another.'

Such was the ideal that Jesus hoped to realise on earth while He should still *be* on earth. What a shock to this hope was the attitude of that crowd in the desert of Bethsaida! They clamoured for a social revolution; they proposed to make Him a king. They had been quite sincere in their communion with Jesus; they had been quite sincere in their communion with one another; but in both cases they had mistaken a part for the whole. Their error was not selfishness; they were quite willing to *pass* the physical bread as well as to appropriate it. Their error lay in supposing that the value of Christ's mission was *merely* physical. Their reverence for Him was deep, but it was based on a false impression It rested on the belief that Christian salvation was first and foremost an external thing, and that the beginning and end of the mission of Jesus was to make a new division of the outward inheritance.

So far, it was only a *little* cloud. The multitude were as yet merely on the threshold; they could not be expected to have reached high spiritual views. But a greater blow was coming. Let us follow the stream of the narrative. From the crowd of mistaken friends in the desert of Bethsaida Jesus takes refuge in flight. He feels that the kingdom proposed by *them* is a *travesty*; He is alone in spirit and He longs to be alone in fact. He retires into the mountain recesses where the historian cannot follow Him. His thoughts must have been very sad. The narrative inadvertently reveals this. He has a sleepless night. When others are in the arms of slumber, in the watches of the dark hours He crosses the Sea of Galilee. He joins the band of original disciples—the members of the first league of pity, and those whom they had drawn around them. He comes into Capernaum — the city of His most brilliant triumphs—as if to restore His drooping spirit by a memory of the past. But the pertinacious crowd will not leave Him. They follow in His track; they trace Him to the synagogue of Capernaum; they surround Him there; the experience of the desert is repeated in the city. Jesus faces them with words of stern rebuke. He tells them He is not deceived by their homage. He tells them He is quite aware they are seeking Him for *less* than the highest gift He has to bestow. And then, passing from rebuke to exhortation, He delivers to them one of the most remarkable sermons on record. I should call it the third epoch-making sermon of His life. The first was at Nazareth; the second was on the summit of Hermon; this was in the synagogue of Capernaum.

It was a singular scene for a discourse like this. The subject of the sermon was the power of the internal. One would think the last place for such a theme would be a crowded assembly. But I often find Jesus choosing localities by contrast. The Sermon on the Mount consists of precepts which are only applicable to the *plain*; the sermon in the city of Capernaum consists of precepts which are only applicable to the *mount*. In the one,

Jesus stands *above* the world and tells men how to live below ; in the other, Jesus stands in the *midst* of the world and tells men how to live above.

I think the scope of this latter sermon has been often misunderstood. It contains a mass of doctrine ; but this is parenthetical, incidental. The main point is this, 'heavenly bread is better than earthly bread ; the things of the spirit are more valuable than the things of the flesh.' Let me try for a moment to exhibit the sequence of the passage ; it will be found in St. John vi. 22-65. Jesus says : 'You have erred in your selection of diet. You have preferred the outward bread ; the inward is more nourishing. If you want *lasting* happiness, you must be fed from within. Life's outward privileges can only relieve *symptoms*; they do not cure the actual unrest. If you desire lasting happiness, everlasting happiness, happiness that will raise you up even at the day of extremity, you must get, not new privileges, but new life. I am come to give you this new life—this inner bread.'

But so materialised are that multitude that they mistake His meaning. The only notion they can form of inward bread is that of outward bread coming down from heaven. They interrupt the sermon—a fact which itself shows how heated they are. 'Oh!' they cry, 'we shall be delighted. You are speaking of the manna which Moses brought down from God—that manna which gave equal privileges to all. And you tell us you are going to renew that blessed shower. Will you not favour us with an instalment *now*? It would be a pledge, a sign, a foretaste of the glory to come.' It was no sarcasm, it was no mockery; it was the utterance of a sober wish; and *there* lay its saddest feature. Mockery would have been a sin against the *Son of Man*; but this crudeness of the multitude was an inability to appreciate the *Holy Ghost*.

Jesus answers: 'It is not the coming down from heaven that makes the difference; it is the nature of the descending object. Moses did not give you the kind of bread from heaven which *I* offer you. His manna, indeed, came from God — as everything else comes from God.   But the gifts of the Father are not all equally durable; some are for an hour, others are for eternity.   The manna which Moses gave you was from above, but it was only for the hour; it was meant for the periodic support of the *old* life.   But the bread which *I* give you—which is *also* from above— has a ground of distinction based not on space but on time.   It is not meant simply to sustain the old life.   It is itself *new* life—" life more abundant."   Your fathers did eat the old manna and are dead; it could not keep them alive amid the tear and wear of the desert. But the bread which *I* offer you will be life-giving, strengthening.   It will sustain your steps in weariness, it will keep your feet from falling, it will prevent your heart from sinking; it will raise you up even at the death hour.'

Such was the subject of the sermon.   Its subject was its sting.   That which startled the audience was not Christ's declaration that He was the bread from heaven; it was His declaration that the bread from heaven was different from the physical manna. They felt like men who had asked a coin and had received a tract. What was this impalpable thing they were promised? Had anybody seen it? had anybody weighed it? had anybody measured it? Did it add to the *size*? Did it intensify the strength? Did it increase the social position? Had it any mercantile value, any political value? If not, what was the use of it? what was the gain of it? *So* they asked with ever increasing murmurs. From time to time the sermon was interrupted. Then came a novel experience. On former occasions we are always told 'He sent the multitude away'; here the multitude *go* away. Slowly but surely the house empties itself. One by one the listeners drop out of the synagogue. The multitude that had followed from the desert disperse. But that is not the deepest disappointment. If the secession had been confined to the converts of yesterday it could have been explained on the ground of their immaturity. But it was not confined to them. Amongst the deserters were converts of an earlier day—men who had promised better things, 'from that time forth many of His *disciples* went back and walked no more with Him.' Jesus felt as if His work was about to be torn up from the foundation. There is a whole world of despair in the question He addressed to the original Twelve, 'Will ye *also* go away?'

But what *is* the despair? Do you imagine it is the grief of a once popular preacher for the decline of his popularity? You must dismiss that from your mind now, henceforth, and for ever. You will never dismiss it from your mind unless you keep fast hold of the golden chain which binds the life of Jesus— His mission for the sake of the *Father*. I affirm that in the whole march up the dolorous way there is not one step of *personal* sorrow. This is distinctively the first step of that march; and it deserves to be registered. Jesus experiences a bitter disappointment. He feels that the world is less ripe for His kingdom than He had deemed. He feels that He will need to abandon His beautiful dream—the dream of remaining to establish a kingdom of God below.

It had been His life-dream, His love-dream. Not for His own glory had He cherished it, but for the glory of the Father. In the unrecorded days of youth He had felt a Divine passion— a passion to make the Father glad. There had come to Him the bold desire to compensate the heart of God. He had entered into sympathy with that heart; He had felt its throbbing; He had experienced its craving. Above all, He had experienced its unsatisfiedness. He had realised how little the world had responded to that heart, how little return it had given. He had felt dismayed, appalled. He had asked, 'Can I do anything to atone —through myself, through others?' It was a bold question; and He had answered it yet more boldly. He had proposed to give His life to the Father to make up for a world's neglect—to go wherever He should lead, to surrender His will from dawn to dark. And there had risen the fond hope that ere the earthly day was done He might see with earthly eyes the founding of a kingdom of righteousness.

And now that hope had faded. He had found that the world was not ready, nay, that His own disciples were not ready. I believe it was now that He first said to Himself—not for the last time, 'I have a baptism to be baptized with, and how am I straitened till it be accomplished!' What does He mean by these words? That He is oppressed by the weight of His own surrender? Exactly the reverse. He means that He is oppressed by the *hindrances* to His surrender. Men will not come to Him, will not think with Him, will not see with Him. They refuse to behold the glory of that which *He* beholds—a kingdom whose steps of promotion are to be altar-stones and whose badge of dominion is to be the bearing of a cross. We speak of the humiliation of Jesus. He *had* humiliation; but it lay not where it is supposed to lie. It is supposed to lie in His sacrifice; it lay in the *barrier* to His sacrifice. Whatever impeded the offering up of His life to the Father, whatever interfered with the surrender of His human will—*that* was His humiliation, *that* was His

straitenedness !   I call this desertion at Capernaum the first step in the humiliation of Jesus.
I call it so not because it exposed Him to the
cross, but because it sought to *divert* Him from
the cross.   It put a wall between Him and His
sacrificial work.   It destroyed the first dream
of His filial love—the hope that now and here
He might raise a holy temple to the glory of
the Father.

AND yet, Thou Divine Man, I am glad that
Thou hast felt this experience of faded
hope.   I should like Thee to share *all* my
experiences.   It would pain me to feel that *I*
had a phase of life which was foreign to *Thee*.
I know what it is to have a withered hope ; it
is worse than a withered flower.   The flower
has had its day and has fulfilled its mission ;
but the day of the hope's fulfilment has never
come.   *I* know what it is to see the fading of
an ideal dream ; there have been to *me* few
deeper bereavements.   Therefore I am glad
that across even *that* river of trouble there is

a bridge to *Thee.* I should have felt a great blank if there had been no communication here. They tell me Thou wert 'tempted in all things.' I bless the Father that the withered dream was one of Thy temptations, because it is one of mine. I bless Thee that it did not wither *Thy* heart, because it will help me to keep *my* heart green. My hope has been *enlarged* by the fading of *Thy* hope. It tells me that the moment of disappointment may be a Divine moment ; it reminds me that the hour of retreat may be the advance of God. I shall gather the faded flowers from the garden of Thy withered dream.

CHAPTER II

THE SECOND HOPE OF JESUS

THERE is nothing to my mind more certain than the *gradual* character of Christ's human foresight. The historian says He grew in knowledge. The knowledge in which He was to grow was the knowledge of His destiny. His mission was to be revealed to Him step by step. The order of revelation was to be from above to below. The cloud was first to be lifted from the height. Jesus was to see His mission as a whole before He saw it in part. I believe the events were to be revealed to Him backward as they were to His future apostle, the man of Tarsus. The end was to be shown before the beginning. In point of *fact*, His first vision was the vision of *glory*. The salvation was seen completed, the kingdom won. The intermediate shades were omitted from the picture. The consummation appeared without perspective. The offering to the Father was to be an offering of unobstructed righteousness. We have seen how there had flashed through the soul of Jesus the ideal of an earthly kingdom of God which He Himself should remain to establish. The last thing had, to His vision, been made the first. To-morrow had taken the place of to-day. The triumph seemed nearer than it was. The grapes of Eshcol had been revealed, not as the fruits of a *promised* land, but as the fruits of a present vintage which was now ready to be gathered.

But now, over this first dream we have seen the cloud fall. Jesus found that the vintage was not ready, that within the limits of His earthly life it *could* not, on natural principles, be ready. This first hope must be abandoned. But abandoned for what? For despair? No, for a second hope. This cloud of Jesus was itself a revelation. His Father was leading Him over the field, not from the beginning

to the end, but from the end to the beginning.
The last had come first—the vision of final
glory.   The falling of the cloud over that
glory was not a call to despair; it was a call
to see *more*.   It was an invitation to accept
a less roseate view, to seek a fulfilment of
His mission in less brilliant circumstances.
The cloud which covered one part of His
sky had *rolled away* from another.   A new
possibility had opened.   At the very moment
when the first hope was assailed, at the very
moment when Jesus was turning His eye
regretfully backward, that eye caught sight
of a line of retreat—a line from which might
possibly be recruited the shattered ranks of
the army of salvation.

What *was* this line of retreat?   I think
you will find a suggestion of its nature in
the very sermon we have been considering
in the previous chapter.   Near the close of
that sermon there occurs a remarkable passage
which is thus rendered: 'Does this offend
you?   What if ye shall see the Son of Man
ascend up where He was before!'   So rendered,

it is made to read thus: 'Are you surprised
at my saying that I have come down from
heaven? That surprise will be taken away
if you see that I have the power to go *up*
to heaven.' In a discourse on the power of
the inward, could you imagine Jesus resort-
ing to such an external argument? I cannot.
Besides, our rendering is not in the Greek.
There is no 'what' in the original; it is simply
'if ye shall see the Son of Man ascend up
where He was before.'

How shall we explain this strange, parenthetical, seemingly disjointed utterance? It is
my opinion that the words were spoken by
Jesus in soliloquy. He was thinking aloud,
and He was thinking of His audience; but I
do not believe he was *addressing* His audience.
There had come into His mind a new suggestion. There had flashed across His heart
another possibility—the vision of a road to
success, less immediate indeed, but more sure.
Let me try with all reverence to paraphrase
the thought which was here uttered unconsciously and in broken speech.

'I see this multitude is quite unable to appreciate any glory that is not a visible glory.   They have been in my presence day by day; they have seen my works hour by hour; and yet they are incapable of understanding a mental influence.   Why is this? May it not be that their very privilege has been against them?   Perhaps they have seen too *much* physical power, too *much* visible glory.   My presence, which seemed so essential to the founding of a kingdom, may be itself the deterring circumstance.   Would not a temporary *eclipse* of that presence be an advantage?   If my life were for a while to become to them a memory, would they not for the first time begin to realise the power of the invisible?   If they were compelled to guide their steps by a mere remembrance, if they were forced to imagine what I *would* have said, if they were obliged to regulate their actions by an appeal to the *thought* of me, if the ideal of my example were to take the place of my audible command — would they not begin to learn that there *is* such a power as the reign of the spirit, would they not at last be ripened for the kingdom of God?'

Such I conceive to be the thought of Jesus underlying this disjointed utterance. It is disjointed because it is only half spoken; the rest is uttered in the heart. You will observe, it is exactly the sentiment which He thus expressed at a later day: 'I tell you the truth: it is expedient for you that I go away.' These words must have had an origin in Christ's *experience*. When you hear a man uttering a rounded sentiment, you know quite well that the sentiment has originated in his heart beforehand. So with that memorable saying of Jesus. It must have been long in His mind ere He could speak it out with such emphasis. When we hear it on that later occasion it is full-grown. It must have been at one time a new-born experience; it must have begun rather by lisping than by speech. Where shall we look for its lisping? Where shall we find the evidence of its mere forma-tive period? Surely here—in the synagogue

of Capernaum! Surely in this broken, disjointed utterance, half spoken, half felt, in
which the human soul of Jesus dimly figured
a new possibility for the kingdom of God!
If you read truly the life of Jesus, you will
interpret His every saying as a word of
autobiography, and you will look to His
past experience for the origin of that word.
Where shall we find a better origin than the
synagogue of Capernaum for the words which
at first sound so strange and paradoxical: 'It
is expedient for you that I go away'!

What, then, is this revelation in the soul of
Jesus? It is something which brings His
mission a day's march nearer home. I am
far from thinking it was anything like a full
disclosure of His mission. There was no
vision yet of the valley of the shadow of
death. There was simply a revelation that in
some form or other His departure would be
expedient for the establishment of the kingdom. In what form that departure was to be
made was as yet not indicated. I think the
mind of Jesus was dwelling more on the *fact*

of separation than on the *mode* of separation.
As I have said, I believe the steps of His
departure were revealed to Him as they were
revealed to His servant, Paul — backward.
What Paul first saw was not the crucified
but the ascended Christ. Even so, if I were
to hazard an opinion, I should say that in
thinking of His departure the inner eye of
Jesus rested first on the last movement—the
Ascension. This would seem to be suggested
by the words : ' If ye see the Son of Man *ascend*
where He was before.' The last scene in the
picture-gallery gets the precedence of all the
others. As the details of His mission passed
before the eye of Jesus they came in reversed
order. A curtain still hung over the visible
cross. A veil yet rested on the sepulchre. A
mist continued to cover the prevision of an
Easter morning. But the latest stage of all
was already glowing in the sun. The Son of
Man had realised that He must *depart*. He
had come to feel that His union with humanity
must be preceded by a break. The heavens
must receive Him ere the time of restitution

could be proclaimed.   A cloud must recall Him from earthly sight before the great longing for Him could be felt by men.   Through all the darkness one thing had become clear —it was expedient for His followers that He should go away.

You will observe that in these chapters I am trying to trace the mental sequence of the Gospel narrative.   I am seeking to indicate why each event in the life of Jesus occupies the place it does, and not another.   We are now coming to a typical instance of the method I am pursuing.   Immediately after the sermon at Capernaum we find an altogether unique event in the life of Jesus.   We find Him in a position never occupied by Him before and never assumed by Him again. For the first and last time He stands in the midst of a heathen community and preaches a gospel to the Gentiles alone.   He passes into the coasts of Tyre and Sidon—the land of Phœnicia.   That is the unique event of His life.   It is His first voluntary passage beyond the limits of Palestine.   I say 'His first

voluntary passage.' There had been an *in-*
voluntary passage ; He had been carried, as
an infant, into the land of Egypt. But this
second transition was made by His own will.
He stands for a moment in the place of His
future apostle—Paul. It is only for a moment.
It is a sudden gleam of sunshine, a sudden
breath of fresh air, vanishing as quickly as it
came ; yet for a moment it is there ; and that
moment is historically indelible. Phœnicia
had received a greater privilege than Egypt.
Egypt had held in her bosom the unconscious
babe ; Phœnicia grasped the full-grown hand
of Jesus.

That is the event ; what is its meaning ?
Has it any bearing upon the present circumstances of Jesus? Had the journey to Phœnicia any connection with the state of mind
in which we now find Him ? We shall best
answer the question by simply inquiring, ' Why
did He go ?' The motive does not lie on the
surface. The incident is introduced abruptly,
and the imagination is invited to try its wings
in flight. Let us obey that invitation.

It is quite certain that Jesus did not go to Phœnicia for the purpose of preaching the gospel. The earliest narrative is conclusive on this point. We gather from St. Mark vii. 24, that He wished His presence in Phœnicia to be unknown. Nor is there any evidence for the common view that the journey to Phœnicia was a flight. I do not doubt that Jesus would have deemed it His duty to preserve His life for the sake of His work. It is not the *duty* that I fail to see; it is the danger. The cloud over Jesus was as yet an inward cloud. He was suffering from the frustration of his *ideal,* not from any actual persecution; I can see no cause for flight. But instead of looking outside, let us try reverently to enter into the *thought* of Jesus. Let us try to photograph the *inner* moment —the experience through which the *heart* of the Master was passing. He had come to a definite conclusion. He had arrived at the conviction that His temporary absence from the world was a desirable thing ; He felt it expedient that He should go away. If a thought like this took possession of the heart of Jesus, it is clear to my mind that He would apply the principle to everything. He would say to Himself: 'If a complete severance from the scene can do so much, might not a partial severance do a little? Must I wait for Elijah's chariot that I may gain the advantage of becoming invisible? Is there no *earth-born* cloud that could receive me out of the sight of this people? Yes. Within a day's march of this Capernaum there is a land divided from it by an ocean of thought— a land of the heathen, a land of the Gentiles. The gulf between earth and sky is scarcely wider than the gulf between Galilee and Phoenicia. The passage from Galilee to Phoenicia would, to *my* countrymen, be like the passage from life to death; it would bury me out of their sight. I will go there. I will try the effect of silence. I will cross the borders into another world. I will let the men of Galilee miss me. I will throw them back on their memory. I will become for the first time a picture in their fancy. I will

let them feel in some measure the love of the
unseen.'

Such, I am convinced, was the thought of
Jesus. The plan was perfect in design.   It
was frustrated by one circumstance.   There
was one thing which had not entered into
His estimate, and the omission redounds to
His glory—He had not realised His own fame.
What failed was the effort at concealment;
St. Mark says 'He could not be hid.'   He
thought He would be obscure across the
borders; He found that His name had preceded Him.   He found Himself in danger of
being solicited to lay the first stone of His
kingdom in Phœnicia *instead of* Palestine!
He could not do *that*; His spirit revolted
from it.   It was not a question of whether
the Gentile should have bread with the Jew;
that was never doubted.   But the question
was whether the Jew should be supplanted;
whether the bread should be taken from the
children and given to strangers.   Was it now
that the parable of the barren fig-tree suggested
itself?   Was it now that a hundred voices

seemed to cry, 'Cut it down; why cumbereth
it the ground?' I do not know. But I do
know it was now He resolved to make another
effort for its fruitfulness—to dig round about
it and give it one chance more. The Father's
time for His departure had evidently not yet
come.   He would not anticipate that time;
He would work while it was day.   If the
cloud refused to hide Him, it must be because
the Father had still a work for Him to do.
He would obey the mandate of the cloud;
He would reveal Himself to the world again.
In what form this fresh resolve appeared, the
following chapter will show.

THOU canst not be hid by *earth*, O Son
of Man!   In vain wouldst Thou bury
Thyself in the shadows of Tyre and Sidon!
Men will *find* Thee there—concealed behind
the secular drapery!   I often think of the life
of great cities as *eclipsing* Thy presence; I
associate Thee more with the desert than with
the crowd.   Yet the city can live without

Thee even less than the desert.   It is vain
for Tyre and Sidon to call themselves secular
communities.   Nothing but Thy Spirit can
make a community.   I can live in *solitude* by
the power of selfishness, but I cannot live in
brotherhood by the power of selfishness.   That
needs *Thy* power, Thy love.   No bond can
unite men but the bond of Thy Spirit.   It is
by Thee that Tyre joins her masses ; it is by
Thee that Sidon unites her families.   They
know it not ; they call their union by other
names ; but *Thine* is their kingdom, their
power, and their glory.   Thou art the root of
all fraternities ; Thou art the source of all
guilds ; Thou art the flower of all brother-
hoods ; in Thee the lives of men become the
life of Man.   Happy will Tyre and Sidon be
if in seeking the cause of their prosperity
they shall behind the drapery find *Thee* !

CHAPTER III

THE SHADOWS OF JERUSALEM

JESUS has formed a great resolve; a new hour has struck in His experience. I believe that hour to have struck while He wandered along the shores of Phœnicia. It is to this period I refer the beginning of this fresh mental attitude. It is described in St. Luke ix. 51 : 'When the days of His Assumption were being fulfilled, He set His face steadfastly to go to Jerusalem.' You will observe the expression 'the days of His *Assumption*.' That is not a synonym for 'the days preparatory to His *death*.' The 'Assumption' is the 'Ascension.' The act of death is still in the background. Jesus is still thinking only of the expediency of His *departure*, of the power which He will exert in absence. What, then, is the thought which turns His face towards Jerusalem? I have said that the vision of death was still in the background. It was not the idea of Calvary that suggested the journey to Jerusalem; it was the contemplation of the journey to Jerusalem that suggested the idea of Calvary. Calvary, when first it loomed in sight, was not an object of attraction. For a reason I shall state in the sequel of this chapter, it appeared rather as an *interference* with His sacrifice than as the climax of His sacrifice; it threatened to neutralise the surrender of that life which He was offering as an expiation to the Father. The vision of such a barrier to His atoning work could never have been the magnet that drew Him to the capital. That magnet, as St. Luke says, was not death but ascension; it was the prospect of exercising the power of an invisible spirit. Is there any way in which a journey to Jerusalem could minister to such a power?

I think there was. For what Jesus says to Himself is this: 'If I am to impress men by my *absence*, I must first impress them by my *presence*; ere they can *remember*, they must *see*.

Have they yet seen me in the full light—the light of the metropolis? What has Jerusalem seen of me? She has had only a few scattered glimpses at Passover times. I have poured forth my soul in the hill-country of Galilee; I have given the burden of my message to the land of my youth. But Jerusalem—the centre and seat of the nation's glory—has had only fragments of my teaching! This must not be. I must not wish to be taken up into heaven until I have left an impress on this spot of *earth.* My life would be incomplete, my ministry would be incomplete, if I did not go to Jerusalem.'

But look deeper. The words imply more than a resolve; they indicate a struggle. 'He set His face *steadfastly*'—the expression suggests resistance. Something must have been *opposing* His resolve. Where did the opposition come from? From within His own soul. I am coming to a very important point. Standing in the great gallery before the Portrait of Jesus, I am confronted to-day by an expression of peculiar sadness. His eyes are bent towards the capital; a new and a wider sphere is opening before Him. And yet, His countenance wears an aspect of inexpressible pain. I stand with uncovered head and ask 'Why?' With deep reverence I should like to inquire into the secret of that sorrow. I gaze into the troubled Face to catch some hint of that which lines the brow with care. Of one thing I am sure beforehand—it is no *personal* grief. He who said at a later hour, 'Let not your *heart* be troubled,' knew *only* the trouble of the heart—the cares of love. I am quite sure that, whatever this trouble may be, love alone enters into it. There is no wounded pride; there is no fleshly fear; there is no individual cloud—this is a *vicarious* sorrow. Let me draw nearer to the Picture and try to pierce the veil.

There is no difficulty, indeed, in seeing what was to Jesus the deterring element in the journey to Jerusalem. He tells us Himself— it was the prospect of death. The difficulty lies in two questions—first, where lay the legal offence in the teaching of Jesus which made

Him *liable* to death? and, second, conceding His liability to a capital charge, why was death to Jesus so deterrent a thing?

The former question has been virtually answered by me in the first volume of this book and in another connection. Without dwelling on the point, let me briefly re-state it. The common answer would be, 'The capital offence of Jesus was His claim to be the Christ or Messiah.' I have shown that in Jewish law this was no crime. A Messianic claim was no heresy. It might be proved to be false, and if proved to be false, it would need to be abandoned; but to *make* the claim was, in itself, no sign of impiety, no trespass against patriotism. When Jesus said, 'I am the Christ,' He did not take one step towards the cross of Calvary. If he had stopped there, He never could have been crucified. The heresy began, not where He said, 'I am the Christ,' but where He asked, 'What *think* ye of Christ? whose son is He?' The violation of national law lay, not in saying He was the Messiah, but in claiming for the Messiah a power which had never been conceded to that office—a power which had always been ascribed to God alone. The forgiveness of sin, as I have pointed out, was not an act which had ever been attributed to the Messiah; it had always been regarded as a distinctively Divine prerogative. When Jesus said in Capernaum, 'The Son of Man has power on earth to forgive sins,' He said something which ran directly counter to the Jewish faith —a faith which placed the judgment of the sinner in the hands of God alone. He had escaped prosecution simply because He *had* uttered the words in Capernaum. Had He spoken them in Jerusalem—in the vicinity of the priests and the temple—He would certainly have had an earlier experience of the visible cross. It was to Jerusalem He now proposed to *go*—to go with the same message of pardon. Could He fail to see the result! The prediction of His death is not one of His miracles; it would have been a miracle had He *not* foreseen it. Had He been simply a Jewish reformer, nay, had He been simply the Jewish Messiah, His prediction *would* have been a wonder; but He was claiming for the Messiah a *Divine* prerogative, and therefore from His country's point of view He was guilty of blasphemy.

All this I readily understand. But the real difficulty comes with the second question. Conceding that the journey to Jerusalem on such a mission involved death, why should the prospect of death have been fraught with such horror in the soul of Jesus?[1] On any view of His person you may adopt, it seems a strange thing. Do you say He had the memory of a life antecedent to His earthly life? Then death should for Him have had no terrors. Do you say He emptied Himself of that memory when He came to earth? Then there remained for Him another refuge —His deep trust in the Father. Do you refuse to look beyond the veil of His humanity? Even then, how was death for Him any worse than for you! There have been men for

---

[1] I am here purposely anticipating what I shall treat more fully when I come to Gethsemane; Gethsemane was not the sudden emergence of an unexpected sorrow.

whom enthusiasm has made death painless—
martyrs at the stake, soldiers on the battle-
field. · Had Jesus less enthusiasm than these!
Had He not *come* to make an expiation to
His Father, to offer His life as a compensation
for the myriad lives *un*offered! Was not
death in the line of that offering! He had
elected to surrender His will to the Father
wherever He might lead. Ought not the spot
most distasteful to be the spot most coveted!
If Jesus is to atone by a sacrificial life for the
self-indulgence of a united world, why should
not the most sacrificial hour—the death hour
—be the one which by Him is most eagerly
welcomed?

I answer: Because that hour could only be
purchased by the culmination of the world's
sin. If it was the hour in which Jesus could
give the highest glory, it was also the hour in
which the world must reach the deepest shame.
When you look at the crucifixion of Christ
you will need to view it from opposite sides of
the gallery. Viewed from each side, its aspect
is very different. On the one side it is the

completed surrender of a spotless soul; on the other it is the completed stage of ‚human sin. On the one side it is love abounding; on the other it is selfishness rampant. On the one side it is something to attract the Father toward the earth; on the other it is something to repel the Father from the souls of men.

Can you wonder that in anticipation Jesus shrank from the ordeal! We speak of 'the offence of the cross.' There was something in the cross which offended *Jesus*. *His* ground of offence was the pain it would inflict on the *Father*. Let me again try reverently to paraphrase the thought of Jesus. It was somewhat like this: 'I am going to Jerusalem for the sake of my Father's kingdom. I know that my message to Jerusalem will involve death; yet, for the sake of the kingdom, I am willing to go. I know that this willingness must be dear to the Father; so far, the cup I have to drink will be easy. Yet it will have a bitter ingredient. There will be something in it which may well mar the Father's joy. He may be glad that I am willing to brave the pestilence; but can He be glad that the pestilence is there! It may rejoice Him to know that a human soul has carried His message into the deadly air; but will that make Him more *reconciled* to the deadly air! Will not my coming catastrophe *interfere* with my work of compensation! Will He be more reconciled to the pestilential atmosphere after it has slain His messenger! He may say to *me*, "Thou art my beloved Son in whom I am well pleased"; but will He not say to the *world*, "Depart from Me, ye that work iniquity"! I should not be satisfied with a *personal* acceptance; I want the Father for my sake to accept the *world*. I could not *live* without companionship in the glory of the Father. I would have the world to behold that glory, to share that glory. I would have *all* to be one with Him as *I* am one with Him. It would be a pain for me to know that the house of the Father was prepared for none but me. The bitterness of this cup of Jerusalem is the sense that my glory will be reached on the highest step of the world's infamy.'

Such is my view of the apparent contradiction involved in the Crucifixion narrative. I believe nothing will explain it but the admission that the prospect of death exerted on Jesus two opposite influences — the one attractive, the other repellent. On the one hand, the surrender to death was for Him the final step of obedience. On the other hand, it was a step that never would have been possible unless the world had made up its mind to crucify Divine purity. I have often asked myself why it is that Jesus, seeking as He did the deepest means of expiation, should, in looking forward, have shrunk from death. And the answer must be: He shrank from death precisely because it seemed to *impede* His expiation—because His crucifixion would multiply the world's sin. Calvary might be on *His* side an act of devotion; it was on the *world's* side an act of unrighteousness. Might not the one counterbalance the other in the sight of the Father? To the Father the devotion *might* be sweet, but the unrighteousness *must* be sad. Jesus and the world were both to be engaged in the same deed; but to one it was to be a deed of glory, to the other a deed of shame. Who could say that the eye of the Father would rest only on the glory and ignore the shame! Who could say that the manifestation of one human love would out-weigh the manifestation of a united world's selfishness! None could say it until the Father should say it. No wonder Jesus shrank from death. It was from the world's side what the writer to the Hebrews calls 'a contradiction against Himself'—a contradiction to His work of atonement. The vision of Jerusalem could bring nothing but pain to Jesus.

And yet, to Jerusalem He was resolved to go. Do not think He solved the problem before He made His resolution. Do not think he waited to receive light from His Father. What He did receive was a pointing of the Father's hand. The Father's hand pointed through the darkness, and His voice said, 'Go.' There was no clearing of the air. There was no light seen in the valley. There was no cessation of struggle in the soul of

Jesus. There was simply the imperative call of duty. His mission demanded that He should preach at Jerusalem; His message made it likely that he would *die* at Jerusalem; His dying at Jerusalem seemed to threaten the success of His reconciling work. These were the facts—each equally present to His mind. The duty and the darkness appeared to pull opposite ways; and both drew by a cord of unselfishness. If He *sought* the scene of death it was for love; if He *recoiled* from the scene of death it was also for love. He saw no *solution* of the problem; but He did not therefore suspend His action. When duty and darkness speak on opposite sides there is no question which should be obeyed. Jesus did not hesitate a moment. He heard duty calling in the night, and He declined to wait for the dawn. The call of circumstances was to Him the will of the Father; and He had promised to follow that Will wherever it might lead. He would keep His face steadfastly towards the night blast; He would go to Jerusalem.

FOR me, too, O Christ, there are hours like Thine. There are hours when duty says 'Go,' and when darkness seems to cry 'Stay.' At such times I often pray that I may have light before I go. I sit by the warm fire waiting for the dawn; I say, 'When *morning* comes, I will obey.' And while I am waiting the gate is shut, the opportunity gone. Let me take my steps from *Thee*! Let me be all ear, no eye! Let me disregard the night; let me consider only the call! If I hear the voice of the Lord God in the garden, let it be enough for me! Though I see no flower of Paradise, though I view no Tree of Life, though I behold on the way to Jerusalem no river of Thy pleasures, let Thy voice be enough for me! Let me arise without sight of the flower; let me depart without vision of the Tree; let me take my journey through a dry, parched land—if only the Voice calls me! Let it be enough for me that the Lord is my Shepherd! Though I start not from pastures green, though I journey not by waters quiet, though I see the valley of the shadow of death before me—I shall refuse to turn back if I hear the Shepherd's call.

CHAPTER IV

THE PROGRESS TOWARDS JERUSALEM

To the spectator in the gallery the title I have given to this chapter might seem very strange. I have called it 'the *Progress towards Jerusalem*'; yet, to the eye of him who looks only on the surface, the face of Jesus at this time is turned *away from* Jerusalem. He has decided to go—to brave the death for the sake of the kingdom. And yet, when He rises to depart, He moves in exactly the opposite direction. Geographically speaking, Jesus never went so far away from Jerusalem as at the date we have fixed for His determination to *go* there. Instead of moving south, He advances northward. He extends His sojourn in Phœnicia. He wanders along the shores of the Mediterranean; He looks towards the Isles of the Gentiles. In His return journey

44

He lingers in the north parts of Galilee—the heathen parts of Galilee. He crosses the ridges of Hermon. He visits the most obscure and neglected villages. He comes to Cæsarea Philippi—the most un-Jewish town in Palestine, the borderland between the Israelite and the heathen. This is a *remarkable* journey—unique in the life of Jesus. How shall we explain it at the stage where we have placed it? How shall we reconcile it with the fact that the leading thought in the mind of Jesus was a resolve to go to Jerusalem?

I answer: The progress I am tracing is not a geographical progress. It is a progress of mental preparation. Geography has nothing to do with it. Jerusalem was for Jesus the seat of death; that was its only significance. To prepare for Jerusalem was to prepare for death. Every step of mental reconciliation was a step of progress. It mattered not where the *feet* of Jesus should travel; the one question was, Where was His *mind* going? We must measure his progress to Jerusalem by no *physical* standard. Many a man draws

mentally near his home by the very act of
going away from it. The question is not
where Jesus went in the *flesh*, but where He
went in the *spirit*. We want to know whether
the thought of approaching death can be traced
in the selection of those scenes through which
He passed. It is not alone when walking in
the *graveyard* that a man can show his consciousness of the valley of the shadow. Jesus
was not on the physical road to Jerusalem ;
but was He on the mental road? Had He
taken up His cross into His *heart?* Had His
mind become daily permeated with the thought
of that great catastrophe which lay before
Him? Then we shall expect to find, and we
shall find, the evidence of that permeation—
not in approximating milestones, not in ever
increasing nearness to the cemetery, but in
thoughts which regulate His choice of localities
far away.

Is there, then, any connection between
Christ's preparation of the soul for death
and His contemporaneous intercourse with
places wholly or partially heathen? I think

there is. Why did He penetrate so far into Phœnicia? Why did He walk by the waves of the Mediterranean and look towards the Isles of the Gentiles? Because He had said to Himself, 'I want to think, not of men, but of Man—Man universal, Man cosmopolitan.' And why had He said this? Because He had been confronted by the most universal, the most cosmopolitan thing in the world—death. For the first time in life He stands face to face with the prospect of a perfect union with humanity. As we have stood in the great gallery we have seen Him step by step descend Paul's ladder of humiliations. We have seen Him 'empty' His own will into the will of the Father; but *this* was not a union with man. We have seen Him take 'a servant's form'; but the form need not be the reality. We have seen Him take the human 'likeness'; but a likeness may exist without identity. Then we saw Him come lower still; He was 'found in *fashion as a man*'—deserted by the crowd as unworthy of reverence; but *that* was not a step of union. We beheld Him descend

still further—'He humbled Himself'; He
abandoned His first ideal, gave up the dream
of His youth.   But even here the strong
Messianic nature might seem to *distance* His
experience from mine.   The same calamity
need not make the same cross; Jesus might
lose His life's dream like me, but, unlike me,
Jesus had the support of a Divine will.   In
none of these steps do we find the perfect
union with man as man.   But we have seen
another and a deeper step uncovered.   It is
not yet taken; but it looms in to-morrow's
sky.   If we would understand the walk by
the blue waters of the Mediterranean, if we
would understand the lingering amid the
heathen parts of Galilee, we must ponder the
significance for Jesus of this one remaining
step—the obedience unto death.

In the first volume of this book I said, by
anticipation, that in the contemplation of death
Jesus for the first time entered into union with
universal Man.   He went below the differences
of Jew and Gentile, Greek and Barbarian.   He
touched the common ground for the meeting

of all humanity. That this was His own view is certain; we have His testimony for it. He declares that by His death He will 'draw all men' unto Him. The words are strongly antithetical. They suggest a contrast between His influence in life and His influence in death. In life, spite of the crowds that thronged Him, He was still but the Son of David. The swaddling bands of Bethlehem were yet around Him; He was a Jew with a message to the Jew. But death was to be for Him a *bursting* of the bands of Bethlehem. The troubles of His life might be Judaic troubles. They might be connected, they *were* more or less connected, with solicitude for His native land. But when He bowed His soul to the thought of death, His interest ceased to be national; it became cosmopolitan. He experienced a sympathy which made the *world* His country. Death is not the *only* thing universal to man, but it is that universal thing which most unites the world. *Pain* does not always unite; every man thinks his own kind of pain the worst. *Joy* does not always unite; the possession which gladdens *you* may bring with it no joy to *me*. But death does unite. Death is not only a universal thing; it is a combining thing. The sense of its mystery makes a fellowship. When Jesus felt He was approaching the city of the *dead*, He felt He was drawing nearer to universal Man than He had ever been permitted to do in the cities of *Galilee*.

Is it any wonder that the mental eye of Jesus at this time was riveted on the Isles of the Gentiles! His progress to Jerusalem meant really a progress towards universal Man, for it was a progress towards the great uniter, Death. Is it any wonder that at such a time His thoughts should have transcended nationality, that the branches of the tree should have run over the wall! And now it is, I take it, that there rises in the breast of Jesus that great idea which, at Cæsarea Philippi, breaks forth into speech. You will observe, He is not yet *reconciled* to death; it is only a surrender of *will*. But there comes to Him a thought which, without being a reconciliation, serves as a counterpoise. He will *rise* again. I have said that His human path was revealed to Him backwards. First He saw the completed kingdom; then He saw the Ascension—the expediency of His departure. *Now* there gleams forth the prospect of His return from *death*. Death itself is not yet revealed, not the *glory* of it. But there comes to Him a conviction that He will vanquish death, will rise above it, will come forth from its folds into newness of life. How does this bear upon the point we are now considering? If the thought of death brought Him nearer to the Gentiles, what would the thought of resurrection do?

I answer, it would bring Him nearer still. Death, after all, could only burst the bands of the *old* country; the *rising* from death could give Him a new country, a country accessible to all the world. To rise from the city of the dead was to make a new Bethlehem, a second Christmas Day. Galilee could no longer say, 'He is mine'; Jerusalem could no longer say, 'He is mine'; no *single* nation could hereafter say, 'He is mine.' He would have risen above principalities and powers, above every name that is named by way of national distinction. Men would no longer say, 'He was born in Bethlehem'; they would say, 'He was born on Easter Morning, from the common soil of humanity; He belongs to the city of the dead; we can *all* claim Him.' Men would no longer say, 'He is the Son of David'; they would say, 'He is the second Adam, the Son of God.' Men would no longer say, 'He is of the tribe of Judah'; they would say, 'To Him all the tribes of earth go up; all families of the earth can boast affinity with His Name.'

Is this view fanciful? It is, at all events, not *my* fancifulness. The view was ventilated nineteen centuries ago by the earliest spectator in the gallery—the man Paul. He stands in front of the Portrait; he gazes intently on the Face; then he takes out his notebook and writes down, 'Jesus is the Son of David according to the flesh; but He is powerfully declared to be the Son of God by the resurrection from the dead.' What does he mean?

That Christ had two birthdays—the one local, the other universal—the one in the city of Bethlehem, the other in the city of the dead —the one from the line of David, the other from the bosom of Mother Earth—the one ushering the life into a narrow environment, the other setting His feet in a large room.

I wish now to direct your attention to a circumstance which, before I studied these things, seemed to me very strange. I have spoken of the seemingly incongruous Gentile localities through which Jesus passed on His road to Calvary; I have shown that their incongruity is not real. I must now point to something apparently more incongruous than any Gentilism, because it lies in the mind of Jesus Himself. Let me briefly narrate the circumstances.

Jesus has come to Cæsarea Philippi. He is accompanied only by the original little band —the primitive league of pity. They have clung to Him through good report and through evil. From them He can have no secrets; He tells them of the impending catastrophe. They receive the news as a son would receive

the tidings of a father's disgrace. They are
indignant, remonstrant; they refuse to let
Him travel towards the city of death. It is
not the pain of wounded love they feel—
Jesus has told them He will rise again. It
is the pain of wounded *pride*—the indignation
that their Messiah should *stoop* to conquer.
Jesus does not receive their remonstrance as
a tribute of affection. He turns to their ringleader and says—not to him, but to the enemy
He sees prompting him—'Get thee behind
me, Satan!' To the eye of Jesus Peter is
only an agent; the real actor in the scene
is His old tempter in the desert, who wished
Him at the *beginning* to exchange the cross
for the crown.

Amongst ordinary men nothing helps a
cause like opposition. Jesus required no such
stimulus. Yet the spectacle of worldly pride
here exhibited was well fitted to fan the flame.
It did fan the flame. He breaks forth into
strong enthusiasm, not about His death, but
about His rising. 'I tell you,' He cries, 'that
my empire will not be retarded by this in-

evitable cross. There are some standing here who will not taste of death till they *see* that empire. There are some here who will live to see the day when the faith in me and the love of me shall have become a vital force in the world—a force which must be counted on, reckoned with—a force which will demand the attention even of Roman power.'[1]

Now, should we not expect that with such enthusiasm in His heart Jesus would have hurried to the crucial spot? Should we not think that His immediate impulse would be to direct His *outward* steps toward the city of Jerusalem? Was it so? On the contrary, He waits, passive. It is the most protracted passive attitude of His recorded life. The historian has nothing to tell. Eight days Jesus lingers at Cæsarea Philippi — eight days of seeming inaction, of apparent waste. Jerusalem is waiting for Him, Gethsemane is waiting for Him, Calvary is waiting for Him; still He lingers. Then the eight days are

---

[1] You will observe, however, that this did not solve the question of accepted expiation.

ended; the new week has opened. Surely this will be the *Passion* Week! Surely *now* He will arise and take His journey! He does; but whither? To Jerusalem? No, to Mount Hermon. All the week He has been meditating *this* journey, not the Jerusalem journey. From the league of pity He selects but three— Peter, James, John; and with these He ascends the mountain. Why? Is He flying from death after all? Has He listened to the advice of the disciple who said, 'Be it far from Thee, Lord'? Is He not preparing for the valley! why scale the height? Is He not training for a burden of heaviness! why climb where the air is light? Is He not making ready for the meeting with universal Man! why ascend into the mountain solitude? That is the question which in the following chapter I propose to answer.

MEANTIME, Son of Man, I thank Thee for the revelation of delay. I thank Thee for the revelation that the delay of a hope is no proof that it is not *dear* to Thee. Often I cry for Thy presence at Jerusalem, and instead of coming Thou ascendest the slopes of Hermon. I say at these times, 'What is the profit of my prayers? surely the former days were better than these!' Help me in such moments to stand in the great gallery! Help me to feel that I am only *repeating* the experience of former days—of Gospel days! Help me to see how beautiful is the thought that the delay comes from *Thee*—not from accident, not from chance, not from outward opposition! If I know it comes from Thee, I feel as if I need ask no more. *Thy* retardation must itself be a wing. I have heard the prophet say, 'How beautiful on the mountains are the feet of him that bringeth good tidings!' But *Thy* feet would be beautiful to me even though they were standing still. I should feel the stillness to be a part of the message—a waiting for the ripeness of the message. Only tell me that the stillness comes from *Thee!* The rolling of Thy chariot-wheels is glorious; but the pausing of Thy chariot-wheels is also glorious. All *Thy* pauses are musical pauses; they are part of the symphony. I can say of Thee in the ascent of Hermon, 'How beautiful upon the mountains are the feet of Him that *suspendeth* good tidings!'

CHAPTER V

ON THE MOUNT

AT the close of the last meditation in the gallery I was asking myself a question. It was an artistic question—a study in the proportion of colour. I was asking why Jesus, at the very moment when He was preparing His eye for the grey, should have bent His face toward the gold. I was inquiring why, at the very time of His highest enthusiasm for a cause which involved suffering, He should have sought on the heights of Hermon to experience an opposite feeling.

And the answer I give is this: It is because the true preparation for suffering is not *prophetic enthusiasm* but *present comfort*. Prophetic enthusiasm may be conquered by present calamity—swept down by the torrent of the hour. Nothing can bear suffering but an actual joy; nothing **can** support sorrow but a present comfort. The only preparation for tears is a ripple of gladness realised, not merely foreseen. I have no hesitation in saying that Jesus went up to the mount in order to make ready for the *valley*. There is a remarkable statement by the writer to the Hebrews, 'We see Jesus crowned with glory and honour for the suffering of death.' I should have expected him to say, 'We see Jesus suffering death to be crowned with glory and honour.' But the men who had a front view of the gallery saw differently. They saw that in a deep sense the crown must ever *precede* the cross. They saw that the secret of successful endurance is not the dogged supporting of pain, not the sense of martyrdom, not even the devotion to a cause, but that it is the sight either of a rising, or of a lingering, *brightness*. All acquiescence in sorrow, all resignation in sorrow, nay, all fortitude in sorrow, rests on something *opposed* to the sorrow. A shipwrecked mariner may be kept afloat by the very waters which threaten to drown him; but a heart over-whelmed by the waters of affliction is not kept afloat by *these*. As a psalmist of Israel says, it must have a rock rising *above* the waters.

I shall have more than one occasion to refer to this principle in my remaining studies of the great gallery; it runs consistently and persistently through the later life of Jesus. Here on Mount Hermon we have perhaps its earliest illustration. Jesus has gone up to the Mount to drink of His favourite spring— communion with the Father. He has gone up to get a draught of the sparkling fountain ere He goes down to endure the heat in the valley. He feels that His sacrifice must be preceded by a mental stimulus, a bracing of the heart. He feels that He wants a *crown* before the cross, a glory before the gloom. Like an ancient poet of His land He desires to sing, 'I will not fear though the earth be removed'; but like that ancient poet, He would first walk up the banks of that beautiful river, 'the streams whereof make glad the city of God.'

Jesus, then, stands right below the vaulted sky and communes face to face with the Father. He has withdrawn Himself a stonecast even from the three favoured disciples ; He has yielded His soul to prayer. And as He stands there, as we stand there, we have a strange spectacle—a radiance all from within. There is no increase of light in the gallery. There is no added sunbeam pouring through the panes. There is nothing from without to augment the attraction of the Portrait. Yet its aspect to-day is different from that of yesterday ; there is a diminution of care on the brow. We are left in no doubt that the cause is inward—'As He *prayed*, the fashion of His countenance was altered.' Here, as ever, His glory is from within. Nature did nothing for Him, ancestry did nothing for Him, miracle did nothing for Him, the pressing of the crowd did nothing for Him ; the power that transfigured the world was the beauty of His own soul.

I would not have you think that this was to Jesus a moment of cloudless joy. Remember, it was the cloud that *took Him up* to the

Mount. He went because He felt heavy in spirit. Moreover, the sombreness of His spirit coloured the scene. By whatever name you may call this episode—dream, vision, trance, history—one thing at least is clear— Jesus carried all through it the thought of His earthly burden. Jerusalem was His earthly burden—the dark spot in His future, the dark spot in the future of His three companions. They had all carried up Jerusalem in their *hearts*; no wonder it swam before their *eyes*! Men speak of the New Jerusalem coming down from heaven ; here was the Old Jerusalem coming up from earth! Neither Jesus nor His disciples had left their weight behind. They all had the same dream because they all had the same waking consciousness—the thing to be accomplished at Jerusalem.

That is the gloom of the picture; what is its glory? What is that which transfigures the face of Jesus? Why is Jerusalem's shadow itself eclipsed for a time in light? Is it that Jesus has at last been reconciled to that feature of death which repelled Him? If you say so, you make the future agony of the Garden simply meaningless. I cannot too strongly reiterate my opinion that the revelation of Christ's mission to His own soul was made to Him *backwards*. I have tried to trace the steps of that revelation. Jesus was now being led towards the *final* step—death. He was ready to take it with resignation, but not yet with equanimity. I do not think He took it with equanimity till the close of the Garden scene. Meantime He must progress towards it. How is He to progress towards it? By keeping it in view? No, by keeping *other* things in view. It is not by the shadow of a calamity that I am led to approach the calamity; it is by light outside of it. If you want to understand the comfort of the Trans-figuration, you must put yourself in the place of Jesus where He then stood; you must stand on the Mount with Him. If you do so, I think you will come to a definite conclusion— a conclusion which will clear the present, without obscuring the future, narrative. I am looking at the picture entirely from an artistic standpoint; I am considering merely why it was painted here and not elsewhere. Yet in this limited inquiry lies the root of the whole revelation; and I shall not deem it an altogether thankless task to determine the artistic position of this memorable scene.

I hold, then, that the aim of the Transfiguration scene was to eclipse for Jesus the darkness of death by throwing in front of it a light which was really behind it. That light was the hope of resurrection. If you study the picture you will come to the conclusion that all its tints and colourings are designed to obscure the place of the sepulchre. And first of all I would direct attention to the fact that this is essentially a picture of the meeting of heaven and earth. It is one of those rare days in which the hills seem to touch the sky. Three forms stand on each side of the heavenly gate; and as we look closely there is a strange parallel between them. Within the gate, on the heavenly side, there are three figures—Moses, Elias, and Jesus—the man of law, the prophet of fire, and the Voice of the

Spirit. Outside the gate, on the earthly side, are also three figures—Peter, James, and John. These latter three seem to be made after the pattern of the three heavenly forms. Peter is the lawgiver—the man whose authority is to bind and to loose. James is the prophet of fire—the Elijah of the primitive band. John, in his ultimate development, is the man of the Spirit—the man whose watchword is 'love.' Such a poising of earth and heaven is not accidental. It must have come from an idea in the mind of the artist. And what is that idea? It is what the poet calls 'the bridal of the earth and sky.' It is an attempt to depict on the canvas a meeting-point for the two worlds. Every difference is for the time ignored. Change is ignored, decay is ignored, frailty is ignored. The tread of death is drowned in the sound of marriage bells.

But look again. I am deeply impressed with the fact that every feature of this picture is selected with a view to centre the eye of Jesus on something apart from death. From the great army of the departed, *who* are those chosen to be the objects of His vision? 'There talked with Him two men which were Moses and Elias, who appeared in glory.' Why select *these* from the host of those who had passed from earth? Moses was certainly a representative man. But so far as earthly work is concerned, I doubt if Elijah was. He was in no sense the representative of the prophets strictly so called. He had left no writing; he had bequeathed no pregnant saying; he had achieved no definite result. Measured by national influence Isaiah was a far greater man, David was a far greater man. If the artistic design had been to get representative men to meet Jesus, I should have selected not two but three. I should have brought Abraham to represent the age of the patriarchs. I should have allowed Moses, as here, to represent the age of law. I should have called forth the man who was traditionally deemed the sweet singer of Israel—David, the minstrel and the king—to represent at once the line of the prophets and the line of the sovereigns.

Why is it *not* so in the picture? The answer

is very simple. · It is because the aim of the
artist here is *not* to paint representative men.
That is not here the principle of selection.
What is that principle, then? You will find it
at once if you ask one question. Is there any ·
point at which Moses and Elias resemble each
other? In all points but one they are *un*like.
Moses is meek; Elias is fiery. Moses is
victorious; Elias is baffled. Moses is a
moralist; Elias is a physical wonder-worker.
But there *is* a point in which they are at one
—both are separated from the association with
death. These two men in the tradition of
their country were both dissociated from death.
Moses was without a sepulchre; Elias was
without a shroud. The one disappeared from
human sight on the heights of Pisgah; the other
appeared to human sight ascending in a chariot
of fire. The one left the impression of an eye
undimmed and a natural strength unabated;
the other became associated with the glories of
the sunshine.

Now, why are *these* the men chosen for the
occasion? Because the occasion required these

distinctively. The vision to be presented to Jesus was a vision of resurrection, not of death. Death, meantime, was to be kept in the background; its time was coming, but it was not yet. The eye of Jesus was to be held aloft. When a sailor is ascending the mast, his chance lies in looking up; if he looks down, he will totter. Jesus had begun to climb His cross; He was preparing for Jerusalem. But to climb successfully it was essential that He should look up, not down. His eye must be filled with beauty ere He gazes on the spectacle of gloom. The Transfiguration was the strain of music which accompanied and sustained the march to death.

But look once more. What is the subject of the converse between these heavenly visitors and Jesus? It is expressed in our authorised version by the words: 'They spake of the decease which He was to accomplish at Jerusalem.' But the word in the original is not 'decease'; it is 'exodus.' Why do we render it 'decease'? It is because we have imputed to the men of that time our modern view of immortality—the idea that death is an exodus, or transition, of the soul. Such a view was not then entertained; it came from Jesus Himself, and it came from Him at a later hour. No man of the Transfiguration hour would ever have dreamed of calling death an exodus; no man would have written, ' They spake of His *exodus* ' when he meant to say, ' They spake of His *decease*.' When they spake of His exodus it is clear they were *not* speaking of His decease. They were passing *by* His decease; they were covering the sepulchre from His sight. The *picture* of Jerusalem, as I have said, figured in the front of heaven; but the *burden* of Jerusalem was *trans*figured. Instead of the sacrifice there appeared the *accomplishment* of the sacrifice—its finishing, its result. In the place of death stood resurrection—it was *this* that was called the exodus. And why was it called the exodus? Because it was to lead the children of Israel across a second Red Sea. At present their very reverence for Jesus was a line dividing them from other lands; the Birth at Bethlehem narrowed them.

But the New Birth from the city of the dead would connect them with every soil. It would be to the followers of the true Messiah a second national exodus. It would lead them forth from the captivity of proud isolation into a union with every country. and kindred and people and tongue. It would break the bond-age of a false patriotism by breaking the line of David. It would enable the Gentile and the Jew to claim a common origin for their Lord—an origin which was dependent on no land and which was fostered by no lineage. The exodus of which Moses and Elias spake was a stage of liberal culture that was to sup-plant them both.

O CHRIST of love, repeat Thy experience in *me*! Often am I called to a Jeru-salem of pain. I dare not ask in advance to see the meaning of that Jerusalem ; but I dare ask in advance to be strengthened for it. I dare ask, I do ask, to be taken up beforehand to the mount with Thee. There is none I

desire to be with on the mount but Thee. I
would have no longer a tabernacle for Moses
and Elias there. Thou hast gone beyond
them; Thou hast left them far behind. To
whose experience shall I look but to Thine on
my way to Jerusalem? Thy mount is higher
than that of Moses, higher than that of Elias.
Moses escaped the sepulchre ; Elias escaped the
shroud ; *Thou* hast escaped neither—Thou hast
conquered both. There is no preparatory joy
like joy on account of *Thee*. I shall seek no
lesser mount when I am going to my cross. I
shall pass Moses by, Elias by, Peter and James
and John by. I shall have nothing but a draught
of the *highest* joy in preparation for my pain.
Meet me with the spray of the fountain! Meet
me with the light of the dayspring ! Meet me
with the song of the bird ! Meet me, above
all, with the voice of Thy love ! Let me hear
of the exodus before I enter Jerusalem ; I
shall bear every cross when I have stood on
the mount with *Thee* !

CHAPTER VI

THE EFFECT OF THE MOUNT ON
THE PLAIN

RAPHAEL has a magnificent picture of the contrast between the scene on the Transfiguration Mount and an almost contemporaneous scene which was occurring on the plain. He suggests that while the top of the mountain was bathed in light its base was exhibiting a spectacle of darkness—the spasmodic convulsions of an insane epileptic. And yet, the poising of these two scenes in contrast conveys an impression which is *not* the impression I derive from the great gallery. In looking at the scene as represented by Raphael we are apt to emphasise the separation of the two experiences. It is like the feeling we have in seeing a Parisian funeral—death in the midst of gaiety. But that is not the meaning of the two scenes as they appear in *my* gallery. To me they suggest, not the separation between the mount and the plain, but the *necessity* of the mount to the plain. Let me briefly indicate my reading of this matter.

Jesus, you will remember, only took three disciples to the mount; He left the rest behind. He probably left them behind for their own good—to let them try themselves alone. They had soon occasion for the test. On the day after the departure of Jesus, a man followed by a crowd comes to Cæsarea Philippi, bringing to the disciples his little boy, who was afflicted in the manner indicated. The disciples were nothing loth to try their healing power. They had the fit of empire on them—that same spirit of imperialism which had made them object to the cross of Jesus. They were evidently actuated by no sense of humanity, but by the sense of personal pride. Had it been a purely physical case, the motive would have been of less consequence—although even in physical nursing, a sympathetic hand counts for something.

But in a case like this, involving *mental* irritation on the part of the patient, the want of
compassion was a deadly blank.

The disciples failed.   I can imagine the
laugh of derision at their failure.   It need
not have been limited to the Pharisees.   Many
even of the half-Christianised multitude must
have had a certain satisfaction in seeing the
discomfiture of men who, though no better
than themselves in birth, had yet been put
so far above them.   In the midst of the
laughter Jesus passed by.   He was on His
return from the sight of the crown.   The
Italian painter might suggest that the sight
of the *cross* fell on Him incongruously.   I
believe the entire design of the narrative is
to demonstrate the contrary—to show that
the crown of Jesus was *preparatory* to His
cross.   The key to the whole scene lies, I
think, in the question of the disciples after
they had seen Jesus succeed where they had
failed, 'Why could not *we* cast out the demon?'
They had obeyed all the prescribed rules of
the hospital; they had done everything which

Jesus had done ; yet Jesus had healed where' they had been baffled. They asked, and we ask with them, 'What was the element in Him which was here *wanting* to them?' And the answer must be, 'That vision of glory which He had seen on the Mount.' Remember what that vision was. It was the foresight of a second exodus—the going forth of a prejudiced little band to meet in sympathy with universal Man. In one word, it was the vision of humanitarianism.

Was *that* no preparation for the scene on the plain! In looking on a spectacle of human degradation, can there be anything more stimulating than a previous vision of human possibilities! *Jesus* had seen these new possibilities for man. He had seen in anticipation the exodus of narrow souls. He had seen the emancipation of shallow hearts from the bondage of their own limits. He had seen the prospect of a small life being enlarged, of a poor nature being enriched—of a son of Israel becoming a citizen of the world. Did not such a transformation give hope for all transformations! Was it not greater than would be that of the poor lunatic before Him into the peace of a sound mind! Had not His eye foreseen the exodus of His own disciples from bondage into freedom, from narrowness into universalism, from bigotry into catholicity! Surely the sight of such a wide transition on the Mount might well inspire confidence for the liberation of one soul on the plain!

I do not agree, then, that the scene at the top of Hermon is the antithesis to the scene at the foot of it. I think the vision on the summit was the preparation for the spectacle at the base, and for all such spectacles. So far from *deadening* the tendency of Jesus to stoop, I would almost be disposed to say that it accelerated this tendency. At all events, from the day of the mountain view, His footsteps are quickened down the hill of humiliation. Singularly enough, all the exhibitions of pride come from those who had *not* been on the mountain, who had been left behind on the plain. I believe, as I have said, that they were left behind in order to teach them humility, to let them try themselves alone. They were doubtless the most self-conscious of the company—the subordinate members of a company usually are. Their very surprise at their own failure to heal the lunatic boy indicated a boundless conceit, which would have been amusing if it had not been sad. Moreover, the special election on the part of Jesus had fanned the flame. Three of their brethren had been set on a pinnacle, had been taken up by the Master to the enjoyment of a peculiar privilege. The selection was made for the advantage of those left behind—Divine, unlike natural, selection always is. But the men left behind could not see beyond the hour—could see nothing but the preference. The Transfiguration, for those who had not seen it, was the birth in the apostolic band of the green-eyed monster, jealousy. Who were Peter, James, and John, that they should be thus privileged! Had they done any more than the others! Was the kingdom of God, after all, to be simply a revival of the kingdom

of Caesar! Why should these three precede
the rest! Were they not all as good men as
they! Had not all shared equally the fortunes
of their Lord! Had they not accepted His·
kingdom on the ground that it was to be free
from the subordination of the weak to the
strong! Why *create* a subordination on the
very threshold of the new evangel!

So talked they one to another all along the
road to Capernaum. It was the first exhibition of professional jealousy ever witnessed by
the Church of God. It was at the same time
the earliest protest against the admission into
the kingdom of Christ of the doctrine of
election. The Transfiguration was the birth-
day of apostolic rivalry. That Jesus should
make a selection from the twelve seemed an
unjust thing. That three should be taken to
the Mount and nine left grinding at the mill,
that three should bask in the glory and nine be
kept working in the field—this was something
which had falsified their ideal of spiritual
equality and Christian brotherhood! They
had been quite willing that the twelve should

have been selected out of the million; but it
was intolerable that the three should have
been privileged above the nine!

What they did not see was that in both
cases the favour was intended for those left
behind—that the twelve had been selected
for the sake of the million, the three for the
sake of the nine. Jesus was determined they
should know this; and when they reached
Capernaum He poured forth one of the most
remarkable discourses He had uttered since
the delivery of the Sermon on the Mount. It
occupies nearly the entire space of Matthew
xviii.; but to my mind its nucleus lies in the
single statement, that the guardian angels in
heaven of little children on earth always
behold the face of the heavenly Father. The
idea evidently is that these guardian angels
get their beatific vision in order to make them
stoop. Their exaltation has not the effect of
making them look up, but of making them look
down. They have been elevated to the height
in order that they may bend not merely to the
plain but to the valley—to the utmost verge of

human impotence—to the helplessness of a child. Let me again try reverently to paraphrase the thought of Jesus.

'You think that three of your number have received a special privilege. From a selfish point of view, from *your* point of view, they have *not*. They have been elected not to a privilege but to a burden. They have been taken up to the mount, not that they may rise *above* you, but that they may bend *below* you. Some one is needed to come lower than you have come. You have been lifting your eyes too high. You have been considering that your mission lies with the strong and mighty—with those who can help the advance of the kingdom. I tell you it lies with the child-life of humanity—with those who can give nothing and must receive all. To go down to man in his emptiness, in his unremunerativeness, is a burdensome thing. I have elected three of you to bear that burden —to help you towards your true mission. I have brought them up to a height where they could behold the face of the Father. I have

done so because the guardian angels of little
children are there. It is because they always
behold the face of the Father that they are
always able to *succour* little children ; they can
stoop low because they see so much glory.
This is my hope for your three brethren. I
want them to be humble, more humble than
you are now. I want them to get a capacity
for bending to things below them, and to
become to you, to all men, examples of that
capacity. Therefore I have set them on the
height, bathed them in the glory; there is
nothing which impels to the cross like the
sight of the crown.'

And now, impelled by that same Transfiguration Light, Jesus *Himself* hurries towards
the cross. At last He takes the long-pro-
jected outward journey—the journey towards
Jerusalem. Jerusalem looked less repulsive
since He had seen it on the Mount; the
sepulchre had been hid by the stream of the
exodus. Driven by the glory of the Light,
He departs from Capernaum almost immediately after entering it. He quits the scenes

which He loved the best—the scenes of
Galilee. Again it might be written, 'He must
needs go through Samaria.' The Light on
the top of Hermon was driving Him towards
Jerusalem by the shortest way possible.
Samaria was the shortest way possible; He
must *go* by Samaria. But Samaria has no
well for Him on this occasion; her well is
dry. She could tolerate one bringing a
privilege from Judea to Galilee, but not one
bringing a privilege from Galilee to Judea.
The town on the direct route shuts its gates
on Jesus and His league of pity; Jesus has
to journey by another way. Two members
of the league are *opposed* to this turning aside;
they are for war, fire and sword—the method
of Elijah. Who are these two members?
'Peter must have been *one* of them,' you say.
Not at all. It is the two sons of Zebedee—
James and John. Why did *Peter* not speak?
I will hazard a conjecture. Peter was, of all
men, the most opposed to the Jerusalem
journey. I could imagine a little boy who
was being taken to school for the first time

experiencing a vivid pleasure when the *coach*
broke down. I think some such pleasure was
at the heart of Peter when the Samaritan town
refused to let Jesus in.

But perhaps the mystery to most will be,
not why Peter did not speak, but why John
did. Has the brush of the artist been guilty
of an incongruous colour?   Is not John the
disciple of love?   Yes ; but there is no fire
like the fire of love. It is a familiar saying
that love will go through fire and water for
its object. That is just what John wanted to
do for Jesus. We are, in my opinion, in a
great mistake about the Bible portraiture of
John. We think of him as a sentimentalist,
a dreamer. That he certainly is not. His
very love is the reverse of sentimental ; it is
pre-eminently practical—it is a keeping of the
commandments. John is the man of waiting ;
but there is a waiting which comes not from
vacillation but from its contrary — which is
the result of settled determination and sure
confidence. Nothing tests a man's character
like his letters. We have John's letters. They

are all love; but it is practical love and love fringed with fire. 'If a man say, "I love God," and hateth his brother, he is a liar.' Is that the language of a sentimentalist? Could Elijah himself have spoken more strongly? You tell me that in this very scene before Samaria Jesus rebukes him for the *want* of love: 'You know not what spirit you are of.' Yes—in *our* version; but the words are *absent* from all the good MSS. John did not err by *want* of love, but by love's intolerance. Samaria and John were both intolerant; Samaria was intolerant from pride, John was intolerant from love. Samaria looked into the mirror, saw *herself*, and would brook no rival; John gazed into the face of Jesus, saw *heaven*, and would brook no gates of earth. Samaria would have exterminated all those who would introduce a *larger* sympathy; John would have exterminated all those who would *narrow* the sympathy of universal love. The fire which *he* would have kindled was in the interest of humanitarianism.

TEACH me, O Lord, to tolerate Samaria;
it is the climax of human charity!
Teach me that the summer of broad-minded-
ness is the power to tolerate *in*tolerance! I
boast of my breadth of sympathy; I call
myself a catholic mind; and I deem the
proof of it to be that there is one thing I
have no sympathy with—narrowness. Teach
me that the want of this one sympathy is the
absence of perfect broadness — the one step
between me and heaven! I have tolerated
all doubts; I have pardoned all agnosticisms;
I have condoned all breakings with the past;
but I have had no sympathy with those who
have *clung* to the past. I have made no
allowance for the man who insists that yesterday was better than to-day. I can accept
the open gates of Galilee; but I have no
excuse for the shut gates of Samaria. I shall
never reach that sympathy till I come to *Thee*.
Thou alone art broad enough to sympathise
with narrowness. Thou alone art tolerant
enough to pardon *in*tolerance. Thou alone
art large enough to recognise the claims of

smallness.   Thou alone art high enough to bear with the errors of a little mind.   When I am confronted by the shut gates of Samaria I will come to *Thee*!

CHAPTER VII

THE UNCHASTE LIFE

THE Bible is the most dramatic book in the world. It introduces its characters and its scenes without preface. Perhaps it would be more correct to say that it does not introduce them at all. It does not show us a dropping of the old curtain and a lifting of the new. There is no curtain. You find yourself suddenly, unexpectedly, without prelude and without preparation, in the midst of new surroundings and in the centre of fresh lives. The narrative of the life of Jesus is conducted on the same principles. There is no line of demarcation between to-day and to-morrow. You are at one moment in the streets of Nazareth, and the next in the market-place of Capernaum; and there is no record of a transition from the one to the other. The Book which most professes to be inspired of God has left the largest margin to the imagination of man.

Nowhere is the principle more marked than at the stage of the life of Jesus at which we have now arrived. We found Him preparing for Jerusalem; we left Him at the gates of Samaria in pursuance of His journey. We expect that the next stage of the narrative will be a record of His entrance into the Holy City. We deem that if the approach to Samaria is recorded, much more will be the approach to Jerusalem. But when the next scene opens, the journey is already completed; we are told that Jesus has gone up 'secretly.' We see Him walking the streets of Jerusalem as if He had been there for years. He has already taken His place as teacher, monitor, legislator. We are conscious of a seemingly abrupt change. The man who had wandered depressed under the shadows of Hermon, the man who had seemed to hide himself from the sight of the sepulchre, blazes forth in the heart of Jerusalem into the aspect of a lawgiver—not the lawgiver to an indi-

vidual, not the lawgiver to a league of pity,
not the lawgiver even to the Jewish nation, but
a lawgiver to the race of Man.

And, as we stand in the great gallery, we
ask, Is this the same Portrait? Is this the
same Jesus whom we saw weighted with the
thought of death? Many have answered, No.
Many have said that some after-hand has
touched the Portrait. Not so say I. To me
the change is profoundly natural, the only
thing that would have been natural. When
you speak of an abrupt transition from depression to confidence, you forget what has
intervened—the vision of the exodus. You
forget that on the heights of Hermon the
eye of Jesus has gazed upon the prospect of
resurrection. The sepulchre itself is not a
whit less repulsive ; the thing which He dreaded
in the thought of death remains to Him dreadful still ; but He has seen a light *beyond* the
sepulchre. Not yet has it dawned upon Him
that death itself would be His brightest crown ;
but there has broken on Him the sight of
Easter Morning, and the possibility of a second

worldly birth. Entering by degrees into the full revelation of His Father, He had come to a place where He could rest in hope. It did not guarantee the success of His *present* mission, but it opened up the prospect of a new mission. It suggested that He might begin again under fresh auspices, and that the path abandoned in tears might by a second effort be resumed in joy.

Accordingly, Jesus enters Jerusalem with a new hope in His heart. It is not a hope for the renovation of His present enterprise, but for the inauguration of a second enterprise. None the less did it lend elasticity to His steps and strength to His soul. In the midst of the Feast of Tabernacles He stands in the temple as a lawgiver. In the courts of that house from which He had expelled the buyers and sellers He now appears as the legislator on a weightier matter. On the very threshold of this Jerusalem ministry we are confronted by an incident which has transfixed the attention of the world. It occurs in our version of John's gospel, though it is doubtful whether it formed an original part of that gospel. At all events, it comes from a record of the apostolic age and demands a place in any study of the Portrait of Jesus. It has been said that in the place which it occupies in John's gospel it interrupts the narrative. It does not, at all events, interrupt the stream of the *development.* I could not imagine for it any more appropriate place than that which it now holds in the life of Jesus. Whoever inserted it in its present position must have been a man of great discernment and a mind of deep poetic insight. Let us stand in the gallery and examine this phase of the Picture.

Jesus had for some days been teaching in the temple. He had made a powerful impression on all but the Pharisaic party. There were hundreds ready to receive Him as Messiah; there were hundreds who, without going so far, were prepared to consider it an open question. His Jerusalem ministry had as yet been all verbal; but His words had been very bold. His voice in the temple had been the counterpart of His voice in the desert. In the desert He had been speaking to the working-classes, and therefore He had appealed to man's sense of toil : 'Come unto me, ye that labour, and I will give you rest'; in the temple He was speaking to the intellectual classes, and therefore He had appealed to a different sense : 'If any man thirst, let him come unto me and drink.' Like the invitation in the desert, the invitation in the temple had come with the *joy* of Jesus. It was not, indeed, that perfect joy He had experienced in the desert. It was rather a breaking than a lifting of the cloud—rather a sight of coming dawn than an actual sense of illumination. Yet, such as it was, it was stimulative; and the principle was again revealed, that sympathetic enthusiasm has its ultimate source not in the grief but in the gladness of the soul.

To keep alive this dayspring, to keep alive this thought of resurrection as distinct from death, Jesus goes in the evening of one of these days to the Mount of Olives; He desires in the presence of the Mount of Olives to fan His memory of the Mount of Hermon. All night He spends in imbibing this joy. He returns in the morning and resumes His labours in the temple. Suddenly, in the midst of His discourse, there is an interruption. There is a commotion at the door, and the attention of the crowd is arrested. A party of the Pharisees enter, hurrying into the presence of Jesus the unwilling steps of an unfortunate woman. She has violated the law of female chastity. For such a violation Moses had imposed the penalty of death. That penalty had long become obsolete. But the accusers of this woman said, 'Whoever claims to be the Messiah ought to revive it.' You miss the point altogether, in my opinion, if you imagine that they only wished to involve Jesus in a question of theory.[1] They wanted Him, on the strength of His Messianic claim, to condemn the woman to be stoned. They held, and I think rightly, that if Jesus should

[1] I believe John viii. 6 to be an addition to the original narrative—the explanatory note of an early commentator. I think the original narrative does not lend itself to that explanation. The Pharisees seem to me to have had a genuine horror of the woman.

say, 'Let her die,' public opinion **was** running so high in His favour that the mandate would be obeyed by the multitude. True, He would then be the enemy of Rome, to whom alone the power of inflicting death belonged. But ought not the Messiah to be *independent* of Rome! If Jesus *were* Messiah, should He not rule from sea to sea! Should He not establish the kingdom of Israel on the top of the mountains! Was the authority of Moses ideally inferior to that of Caesar! Was not the law of Moses God's law! If Moses enacted death for the breach of female chastity, was not that at the same time the enactment of Heaven! Why should not Jesus, if He *were* Messiah, revive the old penalty against the morally impure!

I believe this act of the Pharisees was an honest attempt to put the pretensions of Jesus to the proof. They selected for the trial their own field—the field of morality. They said, 'We have grave doubts of the claims of Jesus; but we will give him a chance in the sphere we think the most important—the sphere of social chastity.' I have no doubt whatever that their animus against the woman was genuine. This particular kind of sin was precisely the one from which a Pharisee was apt to be free. There are cases in which Satan casts out Satan; there are men and women who are exempt from certain vices simply through the presence of other vices. A cold, phlegmatic nature would never commit the sins of Robert Burns. This does not justify Robert Burns; but it shows that one disease may be cured by another disease. It is a matter of daily experience that the advent of a new ailment may cause an already existing ailment to subside; there are forms of physical illness which cannot live together. There are forms of moral illness which are also mutually antagonistic. I cannot imagine that the typical Judas Iscariot could ever have been guilty of that form of sin which characterised this woman.[1] The man who could carefully

---

[1] I use the phrase 'the *typical* Judas Iscariot' because, as I shall hereafter show, the prevalent conception of him is not my own.

count out thirty pieces of silver as the price of his Lord's betrayal would never have committed the *mis*calculations of her who squandered life, reputation, respectability, on the sensuous passion of an hour.

The Pharisees, then, were, up to their light, quite honest. They wanted a drastic reform of social morals—a reform which should consist, not in purifying, but in eliminating, the sinner. They were willing that Jesus should peril His claim to Messiahship on the test of His ability to initiate that reform. They bring the trembling culprit before His judgment-seat. '*Revive*,' they cried, 'the hand-writing of Moses—the law of death against unchastity!' And here there occurs a remarkable scene—a scene which has puzzled the commentators. As the accusers are speaking, Jesus stoops down and writes, with His finger, on the ground. What does He mean? The popular answer has always been, 'He wants to show that He is paying no attention.' I cannot accept that answer. It was not a case for paying no attention; it was a case for very

great attention indeed. Jesus had been appealed to as the guardian of social morals.
Was such an appeal to be treated with con-
tempt, or even with the appearance of con-
tempt! The Pharisees had proposed a grave
problem—had, as I think, honestly proposed it.
They had brought before Jesus a matter which
was near to their hearts; was Jesus to adopt
a gesture which would indicate that they were
speaking to the empty air! We must seek
a *better* solution of the handwriting on the
ground.

And I think we can find it. Moses had
written on stone his law of death against
unchastity. Jesus by his gesture said: 'I write
this day another law, a higher law. The law
which I write on this pavement is "none but
the pure can sentence." I demand a new *jury*
for the old law of Moses—a jury of the first-
born in heaven. Shall this woman be judged
by men who have avoided her temptation only
by a counter sin—who have escaped the over-
flow of feeling by suppressing feeling altogether!· She has done wrong to society by

too *much* passion; have *they* done right by too little! Are there no poor around their doors unfed, no sick before their gates untended, no souls within their bounds untaught!' And He lifted up His eyes and said: 'Let him that is without sin among you cast the first stone at her!'

Then there happens a strange thing. The accusers go out one by one. I think they were afraid of the clairvoyance of Jesus— afraid lest He should expose them to the crowd. I do not for a moment suppose they were convicted of hypocrisy, nor that they had been *guilty* of hypocrisy. The sin of the woman had never been *their* sin; their indignation, so far as it went, had been sincere. But it had not gone far enough. They should have asked if their own *passionlessness* had not been responsible for this woman's passion, if their *neglect* of the poor had not caused the poor to grow up vicious. They did ask it *now*— with that blazing eye turned upon them and that piercing glance penetrating them. They asked it, and they fled from the answer. One by one they left the judgment-seat, until of all the actors in that scene there remained but two—the criminal and the judge.

Paul says that the immediate judgment of the soul at death is before Jesus only; we 'depart to be with Christ.' Was he thinking of this scene — the criminal and the judge alone? It is impressive enough for any picture-gallery. It is pure and absolute contrast; night stands starless in the presence of the day. And what is the verdict of the day upon the night? It is a strange verdict: 'You are black; but I send you towards the sun. You are guilty; but I bury your yesterday. You are unworthy to live; but you shall live to be worthy. I condemn you, and I absolve you. I blame your past, and I wipe it out for ever. Begin afresh; try again; start free. You will be judged by deeds to come, not by days departed; go and sin no more!'

And *now* you will understand why I have placed this narrative here, and not elsewhere. Whence this hopefulness of the Great Physi-

cian, who of all others had the deepest sense
of sin's malignity? Why should Jesus have
seen a chance for this woman in the future
which she had not found yesterday or to-day?
I answer, because He had stood on Mount
Hermon, because He had seen the exodus.
He had gazed on the possibility of a resurrection life. He had seen in anticipation a glorifying of the frail environment. He had seen
the glorified body with its glorified prospects.
He had beheld a break in the old heredity—
a new stream of life impregnating and counter-
acting the blood of the first Adam. And there
had risen within Him a great hope—a hope
for the totally depraved, a hope of new conditions even for the dead in trespasses and
in sin. It was this that made the pure Son
of Man more sanguine for the bad than were
the *im*pure Pharisees.

THEREFORE, Son of Man, I come to
   Thee! I will not accept the Pharisee
as my judge. He has never stood on Mount

Hermon; he has never seen the exodus. He has far less hope of me than *Thou* hast. My human judges have no sight of the Resurrection Morning, no sight of the new environment that is coming to me. They do not see my future possibilities. Send them all out, O Lord! Dismiss them from the temple where they stand, accusing! Debar them from the judgment-seat one by one! And when they have all departed, let me stand alone with Thee—the only pure, the only stainless One! Let my night be confronted not by *their candle*, but by *Thy day*! I would have no lamp to search my soul but the flaming lamp of heaven. I shall only be judged in righteousness when I am alone with *Thee.*

CHAPTER VIII

CHARACTERISTICS OF THE JERUSALEM MINISTRY

WE are now called to contemplate the Picture of Jesus from another position. Standing in the great gallery, we are conscious that the hand of the artist has somewhere imparted a fresh touch to the Portrait. Before inquiring into the nature of the touch, let us mark where it has been imparted. It is at the point of the Jerusalem ministry. Jesus at Jerusalem had entered, so to speak, upon a new diocese. I would add that it was also a final diocese. I do not say He never went back to Galilee again; He did go back. I do not say He never preached in Galilee again; He did preach. But He went back and preached just as a minister who has changed his parish may go back to officiate at a service in his former church. Wherever for the future Jesus may be *geographically* — whether in Galilee or in Peræa or at Bethany, He is still in the Jerusalem ministry, and all His utterances are to be interpreted as the reflections and the echoes of that ministry. I shall therefore, in illustrating the new attitude He assumes to man, have no scruple whatever in binding together the words He uttered in different localities.

There are some changes of diocese that inevitably involve a change of teaching. I do not allude to the differences in intellectual culture; I am speaking of *moral* distinctions. The besetting sin of one district is often quite different from the besetting sin of another. Whenever a preacher experiences this, he has to change his front. It occurred in the transition of Jesus from Galilee to Jerusalem. Galilee and Jerusalem had opposite moral dangers. Galilee was in danger of being too broad; Jerusalem was in peril of becoming too narrow. Galilee was nearer to heathen vicinities, and had caught more of the Gentile atmosphere; Jerusalem was enclosed in the heart of the land, and received only the traditions of the past. Galilee was apt to be corrupted by secular influences; Jerusalem was in danger of suppressing the instincts of common humanity.

Now, this I take to be the explanation of a very remarkable fact. When Jesus transferred Himself from the diocese of Galilee to the diocese of Jerusalem His teaching became vastly more catholic. The distinctive note of the Jerusalem ministry is just its catholicity; it breaks over the national borders in a flood of universal blessing. Why so? Was not the air of Galilee more free, more favourable to cosmopolitan preaching? Why, then, is the gospel in Galilee so much *less* cosmopolitan? Why is it there and not in Jerusalem that we get the restrictions about the way of the Gentiles and the villages of the Samaritans? It is because the peril of a community lies where its facility lies. We put the drag on, going *down* hill — where there is a previous tendency to *accelerate* movement. Jesus put a restraint on Galilee and sought to *lift* the restraint from Jerusalem. The one had an element of over-recklessness, the other an element of over-caution. Either element might become a danger; either might develop a barrier to the progress of Man.

I am prepared to show that the Jerusalem ministry of Jesus, by which I mean all the future ministry of Jesus wherever transacted, was professedly a Messianic ministry to the united world. I say 'professedly.' It was always so *implicitly*—in the *thought* of Jesus. But at Jerusalem it was for the first time openly avowed. This was the *sting* of the Jerusalem ministry. Read the eighth chapter of St. John. For a long time I did not understand that chapter. It puzzled me with its seeming irrelevance. I heard Jesus reiterating that He had come from above, that His origin was higher than that of His auditors, that He had proceeded from the Father, got His message from the Father, been sent by the Father. I heard the audience reply that they were quite satisfied with their own origin, that they were Abraham's seed, that they wanted no help from any other parentage, that they had derived from their present parentage all the freedom they ever desired to possess. I heard these two voices, and I asked myself, what does it all mean? I could not see the point at issue. I could not see, either why Jesus should at Jerusalem have been so eager to emphasise His separate origin, or why the men of Jerusalem should have been so eager to rebut it. It was a mystery to me, an enigma.

At last by a single corner there entered a stream of sunlight. One little verse illuminated the whole chapter, and I beheld in a flash the mystery made manifest. The words that lighted me were these: 'I speak to *The World* those things which I have heard of Him that sent me.' In that sentence I saw it all. I saw why Jesus had taken this and no other moment to insist that He was not ultimately descended from *Abraham.* The man who came from Abraham could only have a mission for the Jewish nation. But the life which came from the *Father* must have a message for *all* nations. If he came from the *Father* he might

well say ' I speak to *The World.*'   The man who
has claimed the blood of a heredity.extending
behind the birth of every nation has claimed
far more than a stupendous *height*; he has
claimed an enormous *breadth*; and it is the
breadth and not the height that first startles
the men of Jerusalem. A son of Abraham,
however great he might be, had their own
blood in his veins ; a Son of God, even though
He passed *through* Abraham, had also blood
foreign to theirs. To be the son of Abraham
was to be *their* Messiah; to be the Son of
God was to be the Messiah of all men. It
was not merely to be the Messiah *for* all men ;
this every Jew would admit his Messiah to
have been, for the benefits of the Christ were
to be universal benefits. But if the Christ had
the *blood* of all nations in Him, where was the
significance of the *Jew*! Could he claim any
longer a unique position ! Could he aspire
any longer even to be the distributor of God's
favours to the world ! Had not the world in
that case an equal right to these favours ! He
was not entitled any more to say to the beggar

'Come up into my chariot.' The chariot was
the beggar's as much as his; it was to go the
round of common humanity and take up every
man according to his need. Such a gospel
might be for the glory of God, but it was
certainly not for the glory of Jerusalem. Such
was the thought that wakened the metropolitan
opposition to Jesus. 'Before Abraham was, I
am,' seems politically a very harmless statement. It was, in truth, a statement which, if
admitted, was the death-blow to Judaism.
Once concede that Abraham got his life from
Jesus instead of Jesus getting His life from
Abraham, and you have reduced Israel from
being the possible metropolis of the world to
being but one of the many mansions in the
house of the Father. Abraham could in that
case be still a branch of the tree; but so would
Caesar, so would Socrates. Judea, as such,
would have no Messiah; she would have only
her share in the *World's* Messiah.

Now, this is the doctrine which, in my opinion,
Jesus had long held in His heart, and which
from this time onward He expressed openly.

From the moment He contemplated the shadow of death, even while He shrank from that shadow, He had seen Himself in a universal relation to humanity. From the moment He contemplated resurrection He had ceased to look back to Bethlehem. From the moment He stood on the summit of Mount Hermon He had begun to view the exodus as a present reality — to regard as within measurable distance the day when the followers of His banner should claim all nations as their brethren in arms. And now, from the outset of this Jerusalem campaign the war-cry never wavers ; it is a battle-call to the united earth. It is a war-cry wrung out by present pain, a cry for liberation. The narrow atmosphere was stifling to Jesus ; it caused His sympathies to beat against the cage, and struggle to be free. Nowhere is He so broad in expression as in this Jerusalem ministry. From no spot do His spoken sympathies radiate so widely as from the sphere that would limit them. It is now I hear Him cry, 'Other sheep I have that are not of this fold.'

It is now I hear Him speak a kind word for heathen Tyre and Sidon, remembering, doubtless, some kindness shown to Him in His wanderings there. It is now I hear Him tell an imaginary story of an orthodox Levite and a heretical Samaritan, and boldly turn the balance in favour of the latter. Was this, too, a memory of kindness? Yes—of the thirst assuaged at the well. I know there was a later reminiscence less grateful than that—the remembrance of the shut gates. But in the soul of Jesus the memory of a kindness long past outweighs the memory of an *un*kindness freshly given; and He judges Samaria by her morning light—the sparkling of the well.

But in expounding this phase of the mind of Jesus I cannot stop here. I am bound to go much further, for the simple reason that *He* went further. I have said He expressed at this stage a universal *sympathy*; but He expressed more than that. Jew and Gentile were, to His mind, equal in origin; but, to His mind, they were not equal in advantages. Strange as it may seem, the Gentile had, in

His view, greater facility for becoming a
follower of the new faith. He had so for the
very reason that he had gone more astray.
Every note of this ministry strikes that chord.
The Gentile's claim is not that he is specially
fallen. It is not that one sheep—the Gentile, is
lost and ought to be sought for, that one piece
of money is lost and ought to be searched for,
that one brother has become a prodigal and
ought to be prayed for. When Jesus speaks
of the ninety-nine *safe* sheep and of the elder
brother who *never* went wrong, He is de-
scribing the Jew at the Jew's own rate of
valuation. In the view of *Jesus* the sheep
were *all* lost, the coins all lost, the brothers
both lost; the only difference was that one
sheep, one coin, one brother, was lost in a
farther field. And what Jesus really means is
that the one lost in the farther field was the
most worth seeking—the one which presented
the greatest facilities for being found, the one
which, when found, was ripest for restoration
to the old environment.

That is the thought which dominated this

stage of the ministry of Jesus. The question occurs, why? *Why* should the most erring have been the most promising? Is error a preparation for grace? Are we nearer to the main road the farther we go astray? Does not one feel disposed to echo the words of the elder brother, the Jewish brother in the parable: 'Have not I lived a life of outward respectability; has not my brother lived a life of shame? How, then, has *he* so much more joy? I have never done anything so flagrantly bad; yet for me there has been no music or dancing, no ring or robe, no killing of the fatted calf that I might make merry with my friends. *I* have strayed less far from home, yet *he* has returned before me.'

I shall answer this complaint by constructing another little parable. Two sheep strayed from one fold. They wandered different distances; one went a single mile, the other three. But the one that went a single mile found its way into a very pleasant garden, and, while it lingered there, the gate was shut; the other, which had wandered farther, remained in the free uplands. The result was that the sheep which had strayed three miles got home sooner than that which had wandered only one.

Behold now the interpretation of this parable! The Gentile was farther away from Jesus than the Jew. But the Jew had a barrier to the retracing of his steps which the Gentile had not. The Gentile, however far away, was out in the open. But the Jew had got enclosed in a garden. It was a garden, no doubt, of many beauties, of fine fruits and fair flowers. None the less it was to him a prison; it prevented his steps from returning home. This was to Jesus the bane of Judaism; it was enclosed, imprisoned. No doubt its enclosure was a bit of good soil—far better than the soil where the Gentiles lived. But the Gentiles had no fence to their ground; they could come out when they liked. Not only was the Jew unable to come out; he could not even see out. He had many virtues; but these virtues he believed to be perfection. He saw nothing beyond him, no *need* for anything beyond him. He had started life with a small ideal—the keeping of certain police regulations. And now he had *fulfilled* his ideal. He stood above his own stars. He had nothing more to aspire to. Like Alexander, he had conquered his world; unlike Alexander, he wept for no other. Looking round his narrow field of duty, he could say with perfect sincerity, 'All these commandments have I kept from my youth; what lack I yet!'

There is no barrier to a pupil like the sense of perfectness. No backwardness in education can for a moment match it. *I* may have written tolerable verses, and *you* may never have written *one*; and yet you may be nearer to the spirit of poetry than I. *I* may believe my verses to be *perfection*; *you* may have been deterred from writing by the despair of reaching Tennyson; you may have beat upon your breast and cried 'Unclean, unclean!' In that case it is you, and not I, that have gone down to the world justified. You have been *farther away* than I from the gate of gold; but your *eye* has been upon the gate.

I have been all along *closer* to the gate; but I have been ever looking, not in front, but behind. *My* view has been the retrospect, and it has made me self-complacent; *yours* has been the prospect, and it has brought you despair. Yet the despair has been gold; the complacency has been only brass. *You* have come from a farther distance, but you have reached sooner home.

SHOW me the golden gate, O Lord—the perfection which I have yet to gain! It is not my sense of virtue that brings me nearer Thee; it is the sense that virtue is wanting. I often go to compare my candle with the wax-taper of my brother, and come back rejoicing; I feel as if I were bearing a light of perfect brightness. Lead me and my candle into the *sunshine*, O Lord! Instead of measuring that candle by my brother's taper, let me poise it against the noonday sun—the sun of righteousness! My laughter will be turned into weeping; my light will become invisible. Glorious weeping! happy tears! Who would not have the rays of his self-righteousness revealed! Reveal *mine*, Thou true Light! Burn up my self-complacency with Thy judgment fire! Strike me dumb before the whiteness of Thy purity! Extinguish *my* torch in *Thy* glory! Expose my faded colours in the sunlight of Thy love! My depression will be the tears of the rainbow—the shadow of the house of my Father. I may need to abandon Jerusalem; but I shall be bound for Paradise.

CHAPTER IX

THE ALTAR AND THE HEARTH

I AM now coming to an aspect of the Portrait which must often have struck the artist-student. I have already pointed out an apparent contradiction in the artistic arrangement of the life of Jesus. I have shown that, though the land of Galilee was the land of freedom, the freest utterances of Jesus were given after He left it. I must now direct attention to a second paradox. Galilee was not only the land of freedom; it was the land of home. It contained the home of Jesus; it contained the homes of the first followers of Jesus; it contained the elements of home-life in general. Here the spirit of youth was uncurbed; here the instincts of the heart were unrepressed; here the fireside was more powerful than the cloister. And yet, the fact

118

remains that it is not in Galilee the Portrait of Jesus assumes its most domestic aspect. It is precisely when the home influences are *with-drawn* that the life of Jesus becomes homely. The Galilean ministry of Jesus might have been *expected* to favour a domestic experience. It was not carried on under the shadow of another world; death was not foreseen as its inevitable sequel. It was transacted amid the joys of nature—with the lily of the field at His feet, with the bird of the air overhead, with the songs of the reaper in His ear. And yet, it is when the shadows of another world appear that the home-life of Jesus seems to bloom. It is when Jerusalem opens its gates to Him, it is when the precipice yawns for Him, it is when death becomes imminent to Him, that the heart of Jesus seems to fly nearer to the earth. At the very moment when He hears a call to leave the world He bursts upon our view in the attitude of one to whom human ties are dear. It is then that for the first time He breaks upon our sight as a man of the fireside, a man of the home, a man of the domestic circle—a man to whom the inter-course of earthly friendship is intrinsically precious, and to whom the hour of social fellowship is, for its own sake, dear.

I have entitled this chapter 'The Altar and the Hearth' to describe the *meeting* of these seeming contradictions. The Jerusalem min-istry is the union of these two heterogeneous elements. Jesus is at once the man of the altar and the man of the hearth. Let me glance at each of the extremes. And first, He is the man of the altar. He is standing face to face with death. I have shown in the previous chapter the cause of His danger. He had claimed a wider origin than the stock of Abraham—a special origin from the universal Father. That, on the lips of a Jewish Messiah, was in the eyes of Israel equivalent to high treason. It was tantamount to sweeping away the line of David. It was the assertion that the Jew's Messiah was everybody's Messiah. It was a claim which stripped Jerusalem of its pre-eminence, which robbed Palestine of its peculiarity. It threatened to do for the Jewish nation what the doctrine of modern astronomy has done for the united earth; it made it an atom in the mass.   It said to the land of Israel: 'You need not be proud of your privilege. Your privilege is simply to have had the *first revelation* of a birthright which belongs to every one as well as you. The Gentile *also* can trace his origin to your Messiah. You may shut him out from the line of David, you may shut him out from the line of Abraham; but he can claim his descent by another stair. It has been discovered that your Messiah is sprung from a higher life, derived from an earlier parentage, begotten of that universal Father who is *outside* all national lines. Your wall of separation has therefore no meaning, your fence no significance, your genealogy no triumph. The Gentiles need not come to the Messiah through you; they can approach Him through their own door.'

There, to my mind, lay the imminence of death. The danger to the life of Jesus was not the *mystic* character of His Jerusalem speeches; it was their political character. The

Jews might not have been able to understand what was meant by Christ's descent from heaven, but they could all understand what was implied in it. The philosophy might tax their brain; the politics did not. They knew very well that if their Messiah came from heaven He was not really theirs—the pitcher was broken at the fountain, the line of David was superseded. The precepts of Galilee had involved no politics; the parables of Galilee had involved no politics; but the transcendental discourses at Jerusalem smote the ground. They shook the common earth; they raised a political ferment. And Jesus knew it. He was quite conscious of the gathering storm. He perceived His danger and the cause of His danger. He felt that words like His, falling on the ears of the Jewish nation, could bring only a thirst for His blood. Death was staring Him in the face. How did He regard it? what did He feel about it? Have we any clock to mark the time of day? Have we any record of His experience at this special hour? Are we bound to imagine, to reason, to infer? Is there no chart which can indicate that stage of the mind of Jesus at which we have now arrived, and tell us the precise spot on which our feet are standing?

There is. We have no need to ponder possibilities. There is extant a document of the day and hour—a document derived from the very lips of Jesus. It is the parable of the good shepherd. To me the interest of that parable is the date of its utterance. It is the first direct record I have of the thoughts of Jesus under the shadow of death. I do not think it is His completed thought. Gethsemane is not yet reached; if this were His completed thought there would be no *room* for Gethsemane. If you want to preserve the consistency of the life of Jesus, you must reserve for the Garden a margin for uncertainty about death. There was one feature in death which was very dark to Jesus—which remained dark *until* Gethsemane. He could only die, as I have said, through the culmination of the world's sin. What He feared from death was an interference with His own work of expiation

—the raising of a barrier to the Father's reconciliation with Man. When He spoke the
parable of the good shepherd, He had still that
fear. Death was not dear to Him. Nobody
can read the parable without seeing that He
deemed the facing of it a brave thing. It is
stigmatised as 'the wolf'—as a power in the
way of the sheep—a power so dreadful that
a hireling shepherd will not meet it. This is
not the language of endearment, nor even or
vanquished loathing; it is the language of
strong repulsion. But none the less, nay, all
the more, is Jesus determined not to avoid
death. He feels that the mark of a good
shepherd is to lead the sheep even though
death does lie in the path. That is His
position in the parable. He is not *seeking*
the wolf, does not personally desire to en-
counter it; but He is convinced that the
path on which He is leading the sheep is
the only path on which they can continue to
live, the only one where they will have a
chance of food. For that chance He will
brave death. He has proclaimed Himself the

Messiah of the united world; that is the only
path on which the sheep can breathe; their
one hope of life is there. He will not desert
them; He will not leave them. Let the wolf
come, let death come, let all imaginable horrors
come—He will stand at the post of duty and
the post of danger!

That is one side of the Jerusalem ministry—
its altar of sacrifice. Jesus is preparing for
His hour—the hour of death. And yet, side
by side with this picture, there is another and
a seemingly opposite one—the picture of the
hearth. At the very hour when this world was
fading from the eyes of Jesus, He was entering
deepest into its innermost circle—its domestic
circle. The moment when the clock was on
the stroke of eternity was the moment when
He began to interest Himself in the minutiæ
of time. To the south-east of the Mount of
Olives there lies a little village called Bethany.
It was but two miles from Jerusalem; and
from Jerusalem at the close of the day Jesus
often bent His steps thither. He had made
the acquaintance of the leading family there—

a brother and two sisters. In their companionship He had found what I may call a purely
secular joy. He experienced, perhaps for the
first time since childhood, a delight which was
not Messianic, not official, not connected with
another world, but purely natural, present,
human. He felt in their society the joy of
life for its own sake, the inherent gladness
of the earth, the native glory of the flower of
friendship. Such was the strange anomaly
which strode side by side with the approach
of Jesus toward the sepulchre; it was like
the sound of dance-music amid the dirge of
death.

At the time of which we speak there is a
curious illustration of this lighter phase. It
is an episode recorded by St. Luke, and,
as I think, greatly spoiled by our common
translation. We make it read as something
dreadfully solemn. The testimony of some
of the best and earliest MSS., coupled with a
view of the circumstances in the light of
common sense, has led me to regard it, not as a
warning to sinners, but as a wholesome advice

to hostesses, conveyed rather with a smile than with a frown. Let us look at the incident.

Jesus has just gone out to Bethany to visit the favourite household. He finds that household in bustle. The sisters are getting up an entertainment on His account; but they are not equally engrossed in the preparation. Mary talks and listens to Jesus; Martha is 'distracted in her attention' through arranging the many courses for the coming guests. If the discourse of Jesus was marred to Martha by the preparation of the meal, the preparation of the meal equally suffered from the discourse of Jesus. She feels hampered by the divided attention. She grows irritable, and she vents her irritation promiscuously: 'Lord, carest thou not that my sister hath left me to serve alone!' Remember, if she was petulant, she was petulant in Christ's interest; if she was cumbered with much serving, she was cumbered for *Him*. Her error was not, as our version implies, that she was in need of the secret of eternal life. She loved Jesus; she was loved *by* Jesus: where was her need!

The truth is, even in her moment of petulance, Jesus was not thinking of the need of Martha but of the need of the guests. She was afraid His interests might be hurt by a social fiasco. He reassures her. Let us paraphrase His words.

'Martha, you are anxious about a choice of varieties. Why should you? Hospitality requires not such. Few things are needful to hospitality.[1] Your sister, Mary, has chosen one of these. You think she has contributed nothing to the feast; she *has*—the good part, the inconsumable part. The very fragments of this feast will be as if they had never been. But she who has gazed beforehand into the face of love, she who has entered beforehand into the spirit of unselfish rest, she who has learned beforehand to look at the world in the light of a coming glory, will communicate to the banquet a sweetness and a strength which will not pass away.'

And all this wholesome recipe for the

---

[1] According to many of the best MSS. this is the real reading for the words of our version, 'One thing is needful.'

warming of the natural hearth is given under
the shadow of the altar of death! Is there any
reconciliation of these extremes? Is there
any point in the mind of Jesus where these two
ideas meet? There is. Call to mind what
it *was* which exposed Jesus to the danger of
death. Was it not simply His defence of the
rights of man as man? And where shall we
find man as man—man unconventional in his
thinking, man spontaneous in his acting? Is
it not at the hearth, by the fireside? Does
not the household at Bethany represent the
very opposite phase of humanity to that represented by the temple at Jerusalem? Does
it not stand for man in his freedom, in his
universality? Does it not figure as the embodiment of the natural instincts, of the
primitive impulses of the heart? Does it not
represent that which is earlier than creed,
previous to custom, existent before conven-
tion? The thing dearest to the heart of
Jesus at this moment was the proclamation
of a universal gospel, a gospel which should
leap the Jewish barriers and fall upon the

fields of primitive nature. And where could He find so fine a field as just within the circle of the home, just within that region of human sorrow and human mirth where the natural passions play and the native tendencies are unsuppressed! The union of the altar and the hearth is no contradiction in the life of Jesus; it was for the sake of the hearth that He braved the altar. Bethany was not the antithesis to Calvary; it was the motive to Calvary. He was braving death in the interest of the universal joy; is it wonderful that on His road to the Dolorous Way He should have paused betimes to contemplate that joy! Is it strange that on His path to the altar He should have lingered a while by the hearth!

M Y soul, keep together the altar and the hearth! Nothing helps thy hospitality like self-forgetfulness. Wouldst thou be a hospitable host at thine own board? then must thou begin by being crucified. No man is alive to the wants of others until he is dead to his own. I have often heard inhospitality referred to thoughtlessness. Nay, it is not thoughtlessness; it is too much thought in a single direction—the direction of self. Wouldst thou furnish adequately the table of Bethany? Wouldst thou make it a pleasant feast, a happy night, a meeting that will leave no taste of bitterness? Come, then, and sit first at the feet of Jesus! Come, and fill thy heart beforehand with thoughts of beauty! Come, and empty thy spirit of its pride! Come, and disburden thy mind of its care! Come, and crucify thy memories of discontent, thy regrets for what is not and yet might have been! Come, above all, and be filled with a larger love—the love for humanity itself, the hope for thy brother-man! So shalt thou contribute to the feast something which will be imperishable —a light and a music that will survive the social hour; *thy* contribution will be that good part which will not pass away.

CHAPTER X

THE ATTEMPT TO ANTEDATE CALVARY

MEANTIME the storm was deepening in the City of David. From the Feast of Tabernacles to the Feast of Dedication it raged ever increasingly. Precisely as the teaching of Jesus became more transcendental, it struck nearer home. We have seen that a Messiah with an origin above the earth was for the Jew a political heresy. We have seen that to hold such a creed was to deny the exclusive privilege of the line of David—that it was to open another line, accessible indeed to Israel, but accessible also to all besides. From the Jewish point of view I do not wonder at the storm. The nearest parallel I can imagine to the circumstances of the nation is the first announcement to the modern world of the doctrine of evolution. Man, particularly religious man, was alarmed for his own dignity. His dignity had, to him, always lain in his speciality—in the belief that he had been separately created. The sting of evolution was not that it denied his Divine origin; it was that it denied his *special* Divine origin—that, so far as origin is concerned, it gave him no advantage over the beast of the field. Change the names of the actors, and the problem was the same. Jesus proclaimed the unity of species between the Jew and the Gentile. The Gentile had always been looked upon as the beast of the field. The Jew stormed at the imputation of a common origin. It was no compensation to be told that it involved a common salvation. He did not want a common salvation. I believe he would have greatly preferred an *un*common *retribution*, provided it had marked him out as a scion of the original stock. Christianity was to him what Darwinism is to us—the assertion of a unity of species between two streams of life which were flowing in different directions and which had hitherto been thought to have come from separate sources.

From Feast to Feast swelled the storm. At
last, on Dedication Day, it burst into a roar.
The adversaries of Jesus, who had passed from
murmurs to arguments and from arguments to
invectives, now went a step beyond. They had
kept their best wine to the last. The force of
reason had failed, the force of obloquy had
failed; physical force remained. They began
to gather stones from the causeway. They
said: 'Let this man have the fate we proposed
for the unchaste woman! It is the legal
punishment for unchastity; and has not he
also been guilty of unchastity! Have not the
prophets called God the husband of Israel!
Here is the would-be Messiah of Israel pro-
fessing to annul the union, claiming for every
land a like participation in the nuptial torch
of God! Is not this the teaching of unchastity! Shall the Messiah of our race tell
His country to break its marriage vows, to
deny its marriage vows! If He give such a
message to His country, shall He be allowed
to escape with impunity! We see *now* the
reason of this man's laxness with the woman

of sin. This man is all round unfaithful to the hymeneal altar of his nation. He has tried to deprive that nation of her marriage ring—the ring which selected her from all others to be the Bride of God. What shall be the penalty of this infidelity, this un-chastity, this incitation to religious apostasy? Shall it be any other than the adulterer's doom, the doom of those who rend the nuptial veil!'

And now in the great gallery there is ex-hibited a tragic spectacle, a spectacle which only once or twice has met the gaze of history : pure spirit meets face to face with brute force, and conquers it. In the centre of an infuriated crowd, with bitter hatred in their heart and with deadly missiles in their hand, stands a single, unarmed, defenceless man. Mind and matter were never so completely poised against each other. Not even in the storm on the Sea of Galilee were they so poised. There, the physical forces were unconscious of their antagonist; here, they were directed right against the breast of Jesus. It was a duel between materialism and spiritualism, in which both recognised the issue, in which neither borrowed a weapon from his adversary. And spirit conquered. Why did the crowd not throw the stones they had gathered? They had physically everything in their favour. They were a hundred to one. They had no outward opposition. They were backed by the government. The missiles were actually in their hands. Why did they not throw? Why did they not there and then anticipate the Cross of Calvary? I answer, because they were here asked to do what the Cross of Calvary never asked them to do—to kill Jesus face to face. The Jew had never been able to do that—not in the courts of the temple, not on the brow of the Capernaum hill; nor was he *now* able. There must have been a matchless power, a mesmeric power, even in the dumb presence of Jesus—a power which paralysed the opposing arm, arrested the uplifted hand, broke the sword before it fell. For a few minutes pure spirit and brute force faced one another. The crowd swung

their arms aloft to cast the fatal missiles;
suddenly the missiles dropped, the arms
dropped, the menacing throng fell back, the
concourse seemed to vanish into air, and on
the bloodless field Jesus stood victor, alone.

What did Jesus think about this? It
may seem a wild question, and yet in the
event that follows I think we have the
materials for answering it. Of course Jesus
knew that the averted issue was a mere postponement. Yet I am convinced by what
follows that He was glad of the postponement.
I am not alluding to that sting which death
still had for Him personally, the sting of the
world's sin ; that would have led Him to seek,
did lead Him to seek, not postponement, but
the passing of the cup altogether. If death
were to come to Him *at all*, I believe that
personally He would have preferred it early ;
it would leave Him free to begin His resurrection kingdom. But it was not for His own
sake Jesus desired postponement ; it was for
the sake of His disciples. They too felt His
death to be a sting. It is true, their sting was

not *His.* Jesus feared *one* thing from death, His disciples feared another. His dread was moral, theirs was physical. But just on that account Jesus could *help* His disciples. He was strong precisely where they were weak—in the hope of resurrection. And they were *very* weak there. I believe, if the Day of Dedication had forestalled the tragedy of the Passover, every fragment of Christ's first kingdom would have melted like the snow; the boldest of the original band would have fled, to return no more. It was for *their* sakes Jesus desired more time. He wanted to show them the brightness of death where *He* saw it—the brightness *beyond* death. Here at least was a patch of blue, on which He might teach them to gaze. They could not meet *His* cross, but He could meet theirs. He had still His own darkness; but where *they* were dark, He was clear. It was a blessed division of pain; it left Him free to be the Helper of Man.

And here I think Jesus made an inward resolve, that henceforth His teaching should be more of heaven than of earth. He said, ' From this time forth I will tell my disciples of the life *beyond.*' Do you ask, 'Why so late in the revealing of a truth so precious?' I answer, it is to me no wonder. I would not have any teacher of religion *begin* with the Doctrine of Immortality. Before you tell your pupil to hope for an indefinite prolongation of life, be sure you find out what he is *now* living for. It is not good to hope for the prolonging of a bad ideal; I should say that the sooner a Mohammedan gets rid of his hope of immortality the better. *Jesus* came to men who had a bad ideal; therefore He did not begin by telling them of immortality. He wanted them, first of all, to desire the things in life which are beautiful, glorious. And so He taught them, at first, to love that which was lovely—lovely now, lovely here. He took them up to the mount and showed them, not the Promised Land, but the present land—its features of beauty, its possibilities of blessing. But now the time had come in which they ought to learn that the present beauty is an eternal beauty. As long as they loved ugliness, Jesus would not teach them immortality. But they had come to love Himself; they had fixed their eyes on His Divinely human glory. Would not the vision of immortality have a meaning now! Would it not mean the immortality of goodness, the deathlessness of purity, the eternity of love! Jesus said, 'I will point them beyond.' But where point *from*? Not from Jerusalem, not from the scene where the implements of death were visible. No, Jesus felt that here the minds of His followers were in trepidation; and trepidation is the foe to revelation. He felt that for the moment, and for their sake, He wanted a change of environment. He resolved to withdraw their eyes from the winding-sheet which the metropolis was preparing. He would still make Jerusalem His headquarters; but, using it as a base, He would go forth on circuit. He would lead His trembling followers into scenes more lively and more free. He would tell them of immortality, but not under the dome of death; He would point them to a life beyond, but not within the shadow of the grave. His revelation of the future should

be made to marching music, not on the field
of carnage.

And here it is that I place the *final* circuit
of Jesus—not a few weeks earlier, as many
harmonists do. Here it is that He breaks up
His camp at Jerusalem and again takes the
field. He leads His disciples into Peræa. He
passes with them into Galilee, the scene of
His former ministry. His tour seems to have
been planned on the idea of mental retrospect.
Each step of the journey carries Him farther
back—nearer to the beginning. From Galilee
He revisits Samaria. You will remember how
Samaria had preceded Galilee—how He woke
to human wants by the thirsting at the well.
Farther back still He travels on the line of
retrospect. He comes to the very beginning
of His public life—to the east coast of Jordan.
He stands in the scene of the Baptist's ministry
—where the heavens had opened, where the
dove had descended, where the approbation
of the Father had gleamed. He stands in the
spot immediately antecedent to the scene of
His own temptation, and through whose in-

fluence He had vanquished it. Who says that His motive for seeking that seclusion was flight! One desirous of flight would not have gone there. The spot was not secluded to *Him*. It was full of memories, full of resolves, full of determinations *not* to flee. He *may* have gone to *brace* Himself; He never went to hide Himself. If the idea of security entered, it was for the sake of His disciples. He wanted *them* to feel secure. He wanted to lift their thoughts beyond the earth; and such cannot be done while the cerements of the grave are visible. He felt that the souls of that little band, which to Him represented united humanity, could only be made to soar by being first made to lie down in green pastures; therefore He chose for them the seclusion of Bethania.

And, indeed, all through this journey the teaching of Jesus is the teaching of immortality. Through all His parables of this time there runs one refrain, ' Earth not sufficient without heaven.' The prodigal has spent all his substance in riotous living. Earth can do no more for him; his only hope is a home beyond. The unjust steward in the very midst of his gains has a sense of accountability which makes him feel insecure, which causes him to cry out for 'everlasting habitations.' The labourers in the vineyard who are hired at the eleventh hour have no time to finish their work; they must look for another life to complete it. The beggar at the rich man's gate has had nothing but want below; his life would not be rounded without a rest in the Paradise of God. These are the echoes of the time—the only echoes that will suit the time. Jesus is bent on revealing to His disciples a hope beyond. Every step of His after-course is guided by that design; if you do not keep this in mind, much of what follows will seem strange. Especially strange will seem the attitude of Jesus towards an event which was even now at the door, and whose entrance has gilded with a unique glory the sunset of Christ's work on earth. The nature of this scene in the great gallery will be considered in the next chapter.

M EANTIME, O Lord, I thank Thee for postponing my hope of immortality. I thank Thee that when I was living for selfishness, Thou didst not suffer me to think that selfishness was eternal. I thank Thee that, ere I could hope for endless life, I first had something *worth* living for—the vision of Thyself. It would be no glory to believe in the immortality of *sin* ; the saint would be the man who wished it were not true. But now that I have seen *Thee*, it becomes saintly to believe in immortality. It is saintly to wish that I may enjoy *Thee* for ever. Men say it is my selfishness that makes me wish to be immortal. Nay, it is my *un*selfishness. It is because I want eternally to love that which is lovely— eternally to love *Thee*. Why is it that the tidings of Olivet, the tidings of Thy rising, have been so dear to me? It is because Thou art love, and Thine immortality is the immortality of love. It is because Thy deathlessness is the deathlessness of all beauty, the permanence of all purity, the fadelessness of all true flowers. There is no joy in mere everlasting-

ness. It would not make me glad to know
that the bit of rag at my foot would be a rag
for ever. But to know that love is everlasting,
that peace is everlasting, that friendship is
everlasting, that sacrifice is everlasting, that
Thou art everlasting—this is the saint's immortality, this is the saint's rest!

CHAPTER XI

THE UNIQUE FEATURE OF THE CASE OF LAZARUS

I HAVE now come to that scene in the great gallery which, as I have said, has given a unique expression to the face of Jesus at sunset. Remember, I have no record of the scene but that of the gallery. I am here to study what is painted. I have no right to paint a new Christ; I have no right even to re-touch the Portrait; my position is that of an observer and a recorder. What, then, is the unique feature of this coming scene? It will best appear by telling the story.

On the secluded coast of Judea-beyond-Jordan, Jesus, as we have seen, has been singing one refrain, 'Earth not sufficient without heaven.' He has been teaching His disciples that immortality is necessary to vindicate the glory of God. Let us bear that in mind before going a step further; it will make the further step clearer. Suddenly there comes to Him a message from the outside—from a spot very near the place of danger. It is from Bethany —from the home of Martha and Mary. However secluded Jesus may have been, He was not secluded from *them*; He had left them His address; they knew where to find Him. The present message of the sisters is a very sad one, 'Lord, he whom Thou lovest is sick.' The reference is to their brother Lazarus. They offer no prayer; they make no request; they simply bring a fact before the eye of Jesus, and leave it there.

What does Jesus do under these circumstances? Does He hasten to the bedside of him whom He called His friend? 'No,' says the Picture, 'He continues two days more in the place of His seclusion.' 'Why?' asks the spectator. In soliloquy, Jesus Himself answers the question, 'This sickness is for the glory of God.' I interpret the answer thus: 'I have been teaching my disciples that the glory of

God can only be vindicated on the supposition that there is a life beyond *this* life. I have been teaching in parable how the beggar Lazarus needs a world beyond to compensate for his wants on earth. But here my Father has sent me a real Lazarus to make the subject of my parable. They ask me to go and heal him; I can do more good by remaining. What my Father needs for His glory is the revelation of immortality to man. Hitherto I have only *taught* that death does not end all; might I not *prove* it? If Lazarus be left to nature he will die; I see this as I saw Nathanael under the fig-tree. Why should I arrest the course of nature? Should I not gain more for my Father by letting nature *have* her course? To vanquish *sickness* would not prove immortality; to vanquish death, would. Has not the Father sent this event as the sequel of my teaching here? Is He not calling me to vindicate His glory by a protest in love's own sphere against the *arrest* of love—by a proof that further *life* lies behind death?'

This is the reading I derive from the gallery.

You will observe the point of contrast between this picture and the similar picture of Jairus's daughter. In both there is a delay of the expected help; but in the case of Jairus the delay comes from the intervention of another suppliant, in the case of Lazarus it proceeds from the foresight that a better occasion for help will arise. In the case of Jairus the interruption to the march of mercy, though it had its plan with the Father, was not planned by Jesus; He was simply assailed by a new form of pity. But in the case of Lazarus pity was suspended in the interest of reason. Jesus said, 'I can save these sisters a great deal of pain, but the world will lose thereby a great deal of revelation.' It was an instance of mental vivisection. For the sake of a larger good two human souls are subjected to a pain which might have been spared them. And the larger good was the vindication of God's glory by the vision of a larger life. But for that, the delay was a waste of time. Martha and Mary would as soon have got their brother back from the sick-bed as from the grave. But

the very essence of the picture lies in the fact
that the proposed miracle *is* proposed not for
the good of any individual but for the glorifying of God Himself. It is designed as a vindication of Divine justice, of Divine mercy, of
Divine love, through a revelation of the truth
that to fill up what is imperfect here there is
space and time beyond the grave.

Now, this is the unique feature of the
miracle of Bethany as seen in the gallery at
sunset. It is the only recorded miracle of
Jesus which is wrought exclusively for the
glory of God. In all others a human element
co-operates. In all others the impulse of pity
for man plays a primary part in the scene.
Even the revivals from death are gifts restored
to *humanity*. The widow's son is raised for
the sake of his mother; the daughter of Jairus
is given back for the sake of her father. But
Lazarus is to be raised for something higher
than any family consideration. His resurrection is to be an offering to God Almighty—
I say with reverence, for the benefit of God
Almighty. He is to be raised to vindicate

God's glory. In the view of Jesus, this glory
is dimmed by the failure of man to realise
immortality. The disbelief, or the unbelief,
in a future state is, to His mind, injustice to
the Father. It is the Father who mainly
suffers by such a scepticism. He is bidden
to write His Book of Life upon a few leaves
of parchment. Omnipotence could not do *that*
—just because it *is* Omnipotence. The Book
is infinite, and therefore it cannot be written
on the parchment. To justify God in *this*
world, man must believe in another. I fail
to see God because I fail to see the risen
Lazarus. The risen Lazarus is not simply
the gift to one bereaved family; he is a gift
to universal Man for the sake of the Everlasting Father. Not merely to dry the tears
of the weeping sisters is the presence of this
man to be restored; *they* must be content to
share the *common* joy. His presence is to be
restored in order that, through the open door
which lets him back, Man may get a glimpse
of a garden over the wall and *postpone* his
judgment of the ways of God.

Let us resume the analysis of the picture. While Jesus lingers in Bethania Lazarus dies at Bethany. The message of the sisters has seemingly been a useless one; the prayer implied in it has apparently proved inefficient. It has, in truth, been simply premature. Jesus might have answered on the spot the cry of Martha and Mary; but He wanted at the same time to answer the cry of the united world. Had He intervened in the sickness He would only have responded to the lesser call. When He hears of the death, or rather, when He learns it by His Divine clairvoyance, He makes a curious remark to His disciples, 'I am glad for your sakes that I was not there.' What does He mean? Speaking from the standpoint of the *Portrait*, His being there or not there had nothing to do with His actual power to cure; He could have healed the sickness of Lazarus at a distance as easily as in the sick-chamber; the clairvoyance is only *introduced* to prove that. Why, then, does He say, 'I am glad for your sakes that I was not there'? To my mind there is only one explanation, but it is a very beautiful one. I understand Jesus to mean that, had He been there, He might have been constrained by human pity to grant a *lesser* good. The very sense that His presence was visible in the sick-room and that yet He was doing nothing might have been too strong for Him. It might have overcome Him, surprised His human nature into an act of compassion which would have forestalled and prevented a wider sweep of mercy. 'I am glad for *your* sakes.' The men at His side were trembling with the fear of *death*. They were not trembling with the fear of sickness; physicians might heal the sick. But was there any physician for death! was there any prescription that could arrest the horrors of the grave! Any man who had a prescription for death would be wasting time to write one for disease. *Jesus* had one, and He was glad that He had not wasted His time. He was glad that, since He had a power to extinguish the *night*, He had not spent the hours in sweeping away the clouds of the afternoon.

What was this prescription of Jesus for

destroying the horrors of death? Do not imagine it was something miraculous. He meant to *embody* it in a miracle, just as one may wrap up a prescription in a parcel. But the parcel is not the prescription; I may lose the one and keep the other. In point of fact, I *have* in this case lost the parcel; I cannot reproduce the resurrection of Lazarus. But the principle which Jesus meant to *teach* by the resurrection of Lazarus is still in my hands; and that is the vital thing. It was not the resurrection of Lazarus that robbed death of its ancient horror; it was the new thought which it suggested. The horror of death was the horror of an idea; to remove the horror of death you must change the idea. What was the idea which made death so horrible to the old world—which drove Christ's disciples out of Jerusalem, which impelled the sisters of Bethany to ring their alarm-bell? Let us look at the narrative, and we shall see.

When sickness has ended in death, Jesus breaks His silence. He comes to Bethany— to the house of the two sisters. He finds it crowded with visitors of condolence—men from Jerusalem, men of the party opposed to Him. The sisters are both grieving, but differently; in their fast as in their feast they keep their respective characters. Mary's grief takes the form of stillness; she sits indoors. But Martha is again in bustle—on the alert for what is outside. She discerns Jesus afar off; she comes out to meet Him; and there follows a dialogue which has become historical. If I were writing a 'Life' I should describe that dialogue; as I am only tracing a development, I shall limit myself to one feature. But it is the crucial feature. The meeting of Martha and Jesus is the meeting of two ideas, I might say, of two worlds — the old and the new. There they stand in the great gallery side by side—the age that was past and the age that was coming! The dialogue between Martha and Jesus is the dialogue between the old and the new view of death. It is a transition moment—the striking of a clock to mark that one hour is ended, that another is begun. You and I will stand and listen.

Says Jesus, 'Thy brother will rise again';
says Martha, 'I know he will rise again in the
resurrection at the last day.' 'No,' replies
Jesus, '*I* am the resurrection and the life; he
that believeth in me shall live in the *hour* of
death, shall live in the act of death, shall
never, on one side of his nature, be partaker
of death at all.'

In that dialogue appear at once the horror
and the glory. To Martha death was a suspension of life; and to her that was its horror.
No doubt she believed her brother would be
recreated; but meantime he was dead — a
thing like the clod of the valley. That was
the awful thought. For, if Lazarus were now
dead, the old life could never be compensated.
A resurrection at the last day would be no
compensation; that would be simply a new
Lazarus with an old memory. What men
have wanted in all ages is a completion of the
old life. They have sighed for a proof that
this defective structure can be repaired hereafter in the point of its deficiency. You may
build a new house on the former site, and

connect it with the former scenes; but the architect of the first house has not thereby been vindicated. Jesus felt this. Standing beside Martha and the Jewish idea of death, He perceived that the time had come for the planting of His *own*. He plants it here— almost in the face of Bethany's graveyard! 'Martha,' He says, 'you have a wrong thought of death; I bring you a higher and a holier one. You call death the suspension of life. No, it is the *transition* of life. I am come to tell you, to show you, that the soul need not wait for the last day—that it can rise from the very bed of death, from the very couch of physical decay, from the very first touch of the hand of corruption. I am come to replace *your* thought of *resurrection* by *my* thought of *immortality.*'

And this impregnation with a new thought explains—what otherwise would to me seem very strange—those words of His to Martha, 'If you believe, you will see the glory of God.' One would have thought that what Martha wanted to see was her brother. And doubtless that *was* her desire.   But to Jesus that was not the main thing.   The main thing was not the resurrection of Lazarus, but what the resurrection of Lazarus proved.   Not the fact, but the thought, was to be the permanent possession of humanity.   The fact would pass away; it *has* passed away.   There no longer stands in the midst of us a man who even *claims* to reveal the presence of the dead in the land of the living; Lazarus himself has not appeared after his second death.   But the *thought* abides — fresh, pregnant, powerful. The Jewish belief has exploded ; the Christian has taken its place.   Immortality, as distinguished from resurrection, is in the air.   There is more hope for the reconstruction of the dilapidated human life; we believe more in the possibilities of the glory of God.   Therefore, also, we have more hope in Man.   Charity is born of the faith in Immortality.   Our schools for the ignorant, our reformatories for the erring, have been built upon the empty tomb of Lazarus, for there we first found the prospect of a larger life for Man.

SON of Man, I understand Thy tears in the graveyard of Bethany. Men have asked the reason of Thy weeping—weeping for one Thou wert about to raise! But it was not for Lazarus, nor yet, methinks, for death. It was for the false view men had *formed* of death. It was because the world could think so meanly of Thy Father as to believe that He could extinguish in an hour a life to which He had given the powers of eternity. It is written of Thee that Thou didst enter the graveyard of Bethany 'breathing indignation.' Often it seemed to me a strange sentiment for a cemetery. But I understand it now. I understand both the indignation and the weeping, for these two were one. Men were impeaching the honour of Thy Father. They were charging Him with having given Man a soul, and then laid him in the dust. Thou wert jealous for Thy Father's glory; I appreciate the swellings of Thy heart, I appreciate the moisture of Thine eye. In my hour of sorrow I often reproach those who robbed me of my first faith. Thy reproaches also fell on them; Thy tears fell on *me*. Thy tears were the showers of Thy compassion for my dead hope, for my dim sight, for my buried faith, for my forgetfulness of the glory of the Father. And the shower of sorrow was a shower of blessing; it was the tears of the protesting rainbow in the evening sky. In the hour of my life's despair, ever let such drops descend on *me*!

CHAPTER XII

EFFECTS OF THE LAZARUS EPISODE

THERE were two things which always suppressed passion against Jesus — His close presence and His complete absence. The former overawed; the latter freed from fear. We have seen the influence of each. We have seen Him face to face with the infuriated crowd, paralysing by His presence the passions of that crowd. We have seen Him in the retirement beyond Jordan, equally contributing by His *absence* to still the national enmity. The thing which provoked controversy concerning Jesus was neither His immediate presence nor His entire absence. His enemies were most powerful when He was neither face to face with them nor at a great distance from them, but in the neighbourhood where they dwelt. They could not stone Him in the same field; but they could plot against Him in the next street.

Jesus had now come again within the surveillance of His enemies: He was at Bethany. The storm which had been lulled to rest burst forth afresh. Within a few hours after His arrival strange tidings spread into Jerusalem. It was reported that Jesus had raised a dead man—a man already in the grave; that the miracle had been done publicly, in the midst of a concourse, in the presence of many of His adversaries; that the Pharisaic ranks had been shaken and were passing over to His cause. The matter was deemed so serious that it instantly became national. It had passed beyond the region of private disputation. It was considered a question of life or death for the nation. A meeting of the Sanhedrin was called; and the High Priest sat in council with his brethren.

Before we go a step further, let us ask what was the cause of the alarm. I have often heard it said, Is it not a very remarkable thing that an event which, according to the fourth gospel, caused the death of Jesus, should have been absolutely omitted by the record of the other three? But I must point out that there is a confusion of thought here. Lazarus had nothing to do with Christ's death. No gospel has ever affirmed that the raising of Lazarus was any offence on the part of Jesus. How *could* the reputation of having raised a man from the dead be any offence to the Jew! Had not his own prophet Elijah worn that fame as a *glory*! The *Sadducees* believed in no resurrection, but they never dreamed of separating from those who did. The truth is, the indignation which now burst upon Jesus was indignation for something in the past. The offence of Jesus was the old offence—the claim to an origin which would have given other nations an equal place with the children of Israel. It was the same alleged crime for which they had sought to stone Him a few weeks before. What the Lazarus sensation did was to revive the *publicity* of Jesus. It added nothing to His obnoxiousness. It simply made it more possible for Him to pursue His former course. The dangerous side which Judaism saw in Jesus did not lie in any of His deeds; it lay in His words. But the greater His deeds, the more power He had to *enforce* His words. From the Jewish point of view it mattered little what the deed *was*; the only question was, Would it help the influence of one who was supposed to be a national enemy? The withering of a fig-tree would have been as much deplored as the raising of a Lazarus. If I am jealous of a man, I deprecate the success of his book irrespective of its subject. Lazarus happened to be here the subject; but the *success* was the real sting.

In obedience to the call of danger the Sanhedrin met. And here *we* meet with a surprise. The tone of the speeches is the very opposite of what we should have expected. Bitterness against Jesus there is, and to the full; but it is the *ground* of the bitterness that surprises us. We looked for an outcry in favour of Jewish nationalism; we are greeted instead with an outburst in favour of Rome. The sentiment of the assembly is focussed in the speech of the High Priest, Caiaphas. Let me try to pàraphrase it.

'Men of Israel, it has often been the lot of my office to present a sacrifice of expiation to heaven. But it seems to me a time is coming when we shall need to propitiate an *earthly* power. Rome has suffered much from the insubordination of her dependencies. They have reaped many privileges, and they have been in danger of forgetting them. *We* have not been the least among the offenders. We have for years incensed that proud empire which bears the sway over us. Her eye is on us now as we stand here on the eve of a revolution. She sees things running to an acme. She beholds men intoxicated with this Galilean movement; and what is the work of the rabble she attributes to the rulers. Let us undeceive her ere she strikes! Let us ourselves put down this movement with a high hand! Let us propitiate Rome by doing the work which Rome would propose to do! Let us prove our fidelity by slaying the Galilean leader! It is expedient that one die for the people.'

Now, here is a very striking thing. The enemies of Jesus had accused Him of being a traitor to Judea; they now prefer against Him the opposite charge—that of being a traitor to Rome. Can we account for this change of front? I think we can. As long as there was a chance of Jesus falling a victim to lawless violence, the Jewish leaders strove to inflame the multitude by the cry 'Treason to Israel!' But when they found that Jesus could not be cut off in that way, when they were compelled to seek His death by law, they had to cry 'Treason to Rome!' Rome alone could sentence to death by law, and Rome would never sentence to death for treason against *Judea.* If Rome should be induced to inflict capital punishment, it could only be on the ground that she herself was menaced. It was no offence to her that Jesus thought the Gentiles equal to the Jews; to disparage Jesus in her eyes He must be proved to be anti-*Roman.* That was the object of the Sanhedrin meeting; that was the object of the speech of Caiaphas. It was a cry of danger intended to be overheard. Spoken at Jerusalem, it was not meant for Jerusalem. It was meant to travel to the banks of the Tiber, to reach the ears of the Senate, to penetrate the palace of the Cæsars, to rouse the co-operation of an empire whose very idea of religion was obedience to herself.

The cry of the Sanhedrin was virtually a sentence of death on Jesus. How did Jesus act under these circumstances? St. John says He withdrew into the country districts. Are you startled to hear that He avoided the blast? You forget, He was carrying out a plan, and He had been interrupted in that plan. He had a few weeks before withdrawn His disciples from the scene of terror in order that they might be calm to hear the tidings of Immortality. He had been teaching their thoughts to soar—to look beyond the seen and temporal. He had been arrested in His work ere it was finished; the domestic bereavement at Bethany had called Him back to the vicinity of danger; He had never viewed the interruption as permanent; He had always meant, after discharging His duty to the bereaved, to complete in retirement the education of His disciples. Is it wonderful that after His Bethany work was done He should again have withdrawn Himself! So far from being cowardice, it was the most consummate bravery. Is there any bravery equal to that of pursuing a deliberate plan in the hour of danger! Such was the courage of *Jesus*!

Jesus does not, however, return to the old spot. He seeks, this time, a different locality. He proceeds in the direction of the Jewish wilderness. Do you think it was by accident that He bent His steps thither? I do not. The Wilderness of Judea was the place where, in the morning of His mission, there had glittered before His eyes the king-doms of this world and the glory of them, and where a voice had said, 'Live for *earth*, and these shall be thine.' He wanted His disciples to hear, in the same vicinity, another voice, 'Pass to *heaven*, and these shall be thine.' He wanted them to realise that death was for Him not even the end of earth, and that the true glory of His kingdom was reserved for the time when He should enter into the cloud.

Now, it is a singular fact that under the shadow of this retreat the hopes for the Messianic kingdom blazed out anew. They had been almost reduced to ashes. Nor did it seem that this was the time for their revival. The fortunes of Jesus were at their lowest. He was to all appearance a fugitive; the hand of every man was against Him. And yet it was at this moment and at no other that the mother of James and John preferred the bold request, 'Grant that these my two sons may sit, the one on Thy right hand and the other on Thy left, in Thy kingdom!'

Strange as it may seem, the thing which impresses me first in this request is not its presumption, but its faith. Why should these men begin to dream of the kingdom when their Master had seemingly only the prospect of a grave? I can only account for it on one supposition. Something must have *happened* to raise their drooping spirits, to quicken their sense of Christ's power. We are often reminded that the first gospels are silent about Lazarus. But is their own narrative coherent *without* Lazarus? Does not St. John supply the missing link—*their* missing link? Is not the Lazarus episode the fitting antecedent to this reviving hope? Did the successful prayer of the sisters stimulate these young men also to approach Jesus through the intercessory power of woman? One thing at least is sure —that mother and sons alike must have seen a star in the dark sky before they could offer a prayer of such tremendous faith.

Yet the presumption is *nearly equal* to the faith—would be altogether so but for the ignorance which lay at the root of it, and which Jesus Himself discerned. I do not, indeed, think that the request of the young men was prompted by pride or ambition. I think it came from endearment. It was the desire to be near Jesus—to be ever by His side. Yet the particular direction in which they sought this nearness was startling: they asked to sit with Christ on His judgment-throne—His own throne—the right and left of His throne! I

believe they cared little either for the throne
or for the power to judge the world; they
chose the sphere from its nearness to Jesus.
Many of us in life commit their mistake; we
apply for a post for which we are unfitted in
order to get some benefit outside of it. The
strictures of Jesus are not against their wish
to be near Him. What He objects to is that,
even with such a motive, they should apply
for a post wholly unsuited to their present
capacity, and in which they must exert an
influence unfavourable to the cause of righteousness. 'You know not what you ask,' He
says, 'can you drink of my cup!' At first
sight one does not discern the connection between drinking of the cup and ruling in the
kingdom. But when we come to see that the
throne desired is a throne of judgment, when
we come to realise that the post requested is
the office of rewarding or punishing the deeds
of men, the thought of Jesus becomes lumin-
ously clear. Let me try reverently to express it by my favourite method—that of
paraphrase.

'You want to sit on my throne of judgment. Have you had my experience? I do not mean, "Have you had my experience of heaven?" but, "Have you had my experience of earth?" If *I* sit on the judgment-throne of humanity, it is not because I have been farther *up* than you ; it is because I have been farther down than you. No man is entitled to sit on the judgment-throne of humanity until, in sympathy, he has been down in the dock with the prisoner. *I* have been in that position. My right to be the prisoner's judge is that I have first been the prisoner's counsel. I know his difficulties. I have realised his temptations. I have measured the narrowness of his environ-ment. Have *you* done this? Where have you proved it? Not at Samaria. Do you remember the refractory village, and how you wished to burn it? You were there the two young men out of all the band who most proved your *inadequacy* for a throne of calm judgment. Is it not well your power was not then equal to your will? None can receive the mission you desire who have not first through sacrificial love been prepared for it by my Father.'

It is curious how at this time the hearth moves side by side with the altar; this, like the table of Martha and Mary, is a domestic scene. Jesus is now on the track of universal humanity — of the fireside instincts. The picture in the present narrative is a fireside picture. I would call this the first prayer ever offered to Christ at the domestic altar; it is a mother's supplication for the prosperity of her sons. It was a premature supplication; but did Jesus remember the equally premature desire of another mother—His own? Did He remember how at Cana she wanted Him to manifest His power before the time? Whether He connected the incidents I cannot tell. But I feel quite sure that He looked upon this initial act of family worship as a typical act —an act which every mother throughout the Israel of God would repeat, and which would form in after-time the basis of domestic union.

I THANK Thee, O Lord, that Thou hast consecrated the domestic hearth. I thank Thee that Thou hast consecrated a mother's prayers. I thank Thee for this inauguration of the family altar — its inauguration by maternal sympathy. Help the prayers of the mothers of Israel, of the mothers of England! Teach them to ask for their sons that which is good! Teach them to desire for their children not the glitter but the gold, not the veneer but the value, not the bauble but the blessing! Teach them to believe that their sons will be helped by tasting of Thy cup—the cup of sacrifice! Forbid that the homes of Israel, forbid that the homes of England, should train their youth to expect only luxurious days on earth! Forbid they should ever train their youth to expect only luxurious days in *heaven*! Let them not dream of any land where springs the thornless rose! Reveal to them that to sit at Thy right hand is a painful thing—that it is *Thy* pain, Thy vision of human sorrow, Thy sense of human sin! When Thou hast sanctified the mother's wishes for the child, the homes of our land will be homes of holiness.

CHAPTER XIII

THE ANOINTING AT BETHANY[1]

LET us bear in mind the singular position which Jesus now occupies as He stands before us in this moment of seclusion. In looking at His Portrait at this time we seem to be listening to a duet. His life strikes the ear more than the eye. It seems to be sung in two parts—a minor and a treble. On the one hand it is very near its lowest pitch of fortune. The adherents who had clung to Him through personal love were very few. The Lazarus episode had produced converts, but they had been converts to His power, and would probably melt before His coming fire

---

[1] The earlier accounts of this incident are vague. I believe they are designedly so. They aim at hiding the agency of the Bethany family—probably to screen them from persecution. I think the statement in Matthew and Mark, that the feast was 'in the house of Simon,' is the note of a transcriber who confused the event with the similar incident in Simon's house recorded in Luke vii. 36, *et seq.*

of tribulation. They would say, 'It must have been a case of premature burial; if this man could raise another, he could prevent his *own* death!' That death, indeed, was imminent; and to the eye of the world it was a sign of failure. Even to the eye of Jesus it was not yet a sign of triumph. He saw that He would survive it. He saw that in spite of it His present followers—those whom the Father had already given Him—would be supported and sustained for a second effort. But it still seemed to mar His work for the outside world—to aggravate in the sight of the Father that very unrighteousness which He had come to lessen and to expiate. From the physical side, every step of Jesus had been in the direction described by Paul's ladder—a step downward. His life had steadily but surely descended from the height to the plain, from the plain to the valley. At the present moment He was actually *in* the valley; He was within sight of the common doom of men. That is the lower part of the life-duet to which the ear listens.

But on the other hand, there is a soprano part. You will remember how Paul told us it *must* be so: 'He humbled Himself, therefore God hath highly exalted Him.' We have seen how the valley is the widest sphere, how the wants of the valley are the universal wants. Accordingly, this period of outward circumscribedness, this period of physical seclusion in the life of Jesus, is of all others that in which His gospel most touches the universal mind. Already have we seen the signs of that universality. Already have we beheld Him bursting the limits of Judaism. Already have we witnessed Him projecting a miracle which by revealing human immortality should justify the ways of God to united Man. Already have we gazed upon Him in the enjoyment of the social hour precisely on the ground that the social hour reveals those instincts in man which are the most unconventional and therefore the most natural and cosmopolitan. All this we have seen; and in proportion as the life stoops, we shall see greater things than these. The two voices

are not discordant voices; they are the parts
of one song; they are a duet.

There is one point which has been coming
prominently forth in this period—the ministrant power of Woman. Woman is the cosmopolitan side of Man—the side least affected
by national differences. It is at this period
of sunset that the influence of Woman, like
that of other universal things, bursts into
flower. In the Galilean ministry her influence
was not unknown; Jesus had utilised her
services for His missionary guild. But that
which Woman wanted was recognition in her
own sphere. It was all very well to be utilised
for religious work; but that was not necessarily
a compliment to the sphere of Woman, for it
was really her incorporation in the sphere of
Man. What she wanted was to be recognised
in her peculiar province—not to be lifted out
of that province. Hitherto, within her sphere
she had been rather the helped than the helper.
Her diseases had been healed; her tears had
been dried; but it had not yet been pointed
out to the world that her influence in the

home was a potent force for the kingdom of
God.

With the declining sun this new revelation
came. We have seen how, side by side with
the altar, there rose before the eye of Jesus
a vision of the hearth. In the days when the
sacrificial fire became visible, the domestic
fire began to glitter and to glow; and in the
centre of the temple of home the priesthood
of Woman was revealed. The pictures of that
time are nearly all female pictures—from the
woman who violated the sacredness of her
hearth to that mother of Zebedee's children
who consecrated her hearth to Jesus. Between
them lay the sweet home of Bethany, with its
memories of joy and its memories of sorrow,
and alike in its joy and its sorrow lighting a
holy fire. And to the trophies of that home
there was about to be added yet another, which
was to call forth from the lips of Jesus the
mightiest tribute of gratitude for the service
of Woman which has ever been pronounced
upon her in any land or at any time. It is
the imprimatur on a mere home service;

but that is its beauty, that is its glory; by
that it has consecrated for ever the ties of
family life.

Let us stand in the gallery again and interpret the scene as it is painted. Martha and
Mary make another feast. 'What!' says the
spectator, 'so soon after the death of Lazarus!'
Yes, but the picture is true to itself.   It
vindicates the good taste of the sisters by
reminding us that between the dying and the
feasting something has occurred—the rising
again.   The picture is a consistent unity; it
puts Lazarus at the feast beside Martha and
Mary. What a breach of art it would have
been if Lazarus had been absent—if this had
been a supper over his dust! It would have
been one of the most ghastly portraitures which
the brush of the painter has ever delineated!
The raising of a man from the dead is an act
with which the artist intermeddleth not; it
is beyond the stroke of his pencil. But the
making of a great feast in the house of a
brother, who a few days ago **was** carried from
its portals to the grave, is *against* the stroke of

his pencil; to describe it on the canvas would
be to portray a monstrosity. This feast of the
sisters of Bethany, commonplace as it is,
demands in the interest of art the *presence* of
Lazarus.

It is, indeed, a *thanksgiving* for Lazarus.
There are some whose hymns of praise are
secular songs. Amongst those, methinks,
were these sisters of Bethany. Whenever
their hearts were full of God they rushed into
social hospitality. Their hearts were full of
God now, and they poured them out in the
old way. They invited guests from far and
near to be sharers in their joy. But there was
one whose presence they solicited above all
others—the true object of their thanksgiving—
Jesus. They were not afraid to offer Him a
thing otherwise unconsecrated—an hour of
purely secular hospitality. And Jesus was not
afraid to come—not even from those solemn
shadows of death which encompassed Him.
Did not these shadows themselves unite Him
to that which was universal in Man—below
creeds, beyond nationalities? Did they not

join Him to that want which lies at the root
of human brotherhood, and which causes the
sons of men to gather into social fellowship?
They did; therefore Jesus came—came to
a seemingly incongruous scene.   He issued
from His place of seclusion near the Judaic
wilderness.   There, in the lonely village called
Ephraim—a spot unrecognised by the modern
traveller—He had spent these intermediate
days.   Now He reappears—in the home of
festivity, in the vicinity of danger; and here
is enacted a scene which He predicted would
become historical, and which has actually
realised the expectation.

Outwardly, what happened was a very
simple thing—not the kind of action of which
one prophesies immortality.   It was merely an
excessive expression of personal gratitude.   In
a moment of rapturous thanksgiving for the
restored life of her brother, Mary deliberately
broke a box of the most precious ointment,
and, instead of contenting herself with the
method of greeting commonly received by
honoured guests, she anointed the very feet

of Jesus, and wiped them with the hairs of her head! It seemed a deed of extravagant profusion. It was an expenditure of fireworks—brilliant but evanescent. It was love squandering upon an illumination a sum of money that might have been spent in beneficence; and it awakened something like a thrill of horror. The treasurer Judas *said*, and the other disciples *thought*, 'To what purpose is this waste!'

But Jesus said: 'I tell you this is the most permanent thing that has yet been done for me. You think it a fugitive act, a wasteful deed. It is, on the contrary, a deed that bears the stamp of immortality. Wheresoever this gospel is preached—and it will be preached everywhere—*there* shall the act of this woman be proclaimed. Other deeds record the good done *by* me; this will tell of the good done *to* me. I have influenced the *world*; but this woman has influenced *me*. She hath wrought a good work in me; she did it for my burial.'

I have here followed the form of the narrative given by St. Matthew, because I think the rendering there is more correct as regards the ground of Mary's commendation. Adopting, then, this reading, what does Jesus mean by the words, 'She did it for my burial'? As I have said, Mary's motive was *not* the anointing of Jesus for His burial. That would have been an offering of her *sorrow*. This was unmistakably an offering of her joy. She was thinking, not of the burial preparing, but of the burial baffled. The breaking of the alabaster box was a tribute, not to death, but to life. It was an offering of thanks to God for the restored life of her brother Lazarus. Jesus knew it to be so, and He accepted the motive even while He saw a deeper use for the deed. He put more into the box than Mary had originally put into it; but He did not *refuse* what had been originally inserted. He saw in Mary's action more than she saw herself; but He beheld also the amount *she* beheld. And I cannot but remark in passing, that, to those followers of the Christian faith who are seeking from their Scriptures a solace in the hour of bereavement, I can imagine no greater comfort than a statement of the fact that Jesus once accepted a costly offering as a tribute of gratitude for annulling the separation wrought by death.

But, as I have said, Jesus put more into the box than He found there. This is a case of imputed righteousness. Mary was doing more than she knew. The very form of the words of Jesus suggests to me that this was in His mind. 'Mary, you wish your offering to point back to the vacant tomb of your brother; but it also points forward to another tomb—my own. You have meant your deed to have a bearing on the burial of Lazarus; it has had an additional bearing—on *my* burial. You have meant it to be simply retrospective; it has been prospective too. It has raised issues you have not dreamed of. You designed it for only a village thanksgiving; you have performed a deed which will be more potent in its consequences than all the conquests of Cæsar.'

What, then, was this deed? What was that good work which she wrought in Jesus? If

you would arrive at the answer, remember
what was at this time the deepest thought of
His mind. It was what He calls His burial,
by which He means the coming of death.
Remember that at the very moment when
He was preparing His disciples for the great
catastrophe, there was a side of that catastrophe
which to Himself was still dark—a side of which
He could not yet say, 'O death, where is thy
sting! O grave, where is thy victory!' What
it was we have seen before and shall see again.
Meantime, it is sufficient to remind you that
death for Him had still a valley, still a shadow.
You will remember also what I have pointed
out as the law of man's nature and pre-
eminently a law of the nature of Jesus—that
the best help for a valley and a shadow is a
previous joy. We have seen how it was after
a great joy that Jesus took up the burden of
the labouring and the heavy-laden. We have
seen how it was after a great joy—His Transfiguration joy—that He set His face steadfastly
to go to the dreaded Jerusalem. And now
there comes to Him the same preliminary

stimulus. The devotion of this woman was like a draught of strong wine, like a blast of military music. It strengthened Jesus for the battle. It did not make clearer the dark side of the sepulchre, but it lifted the eye of Jesus to the side which was not dark. It said, 'Your Father has already accepted from you a few flowers which will not wither even when planted on your grave; even in the depth of His winter you have brought some bloom to the heart of your Father.'

Therefore it was that Jesus said, 'She has done me good; she has strengthened me for my burial.' She had not His burial in her mind; but without meaning it she braced Him for His destiny. Without such gleams of light Jesus would have broken down before the time; we shall prove this in the sequel. Without such gleams of light we should *all* break down before the time. We do not reach our destiny by the strength with which we started; we should never come near the goal but for the alabaster boxes which, by seeming accident, meet us on the way. No

wonder Jesus imputes to this box more than
was in it! There was in it only the grateful
devotion of a single human soul; but on the
strength of that devotion Jesus walked for
many hours. It propped up His sinking frame
—sinking all the faster because it was carrying a burden unseen. It spoke a word of
recognition to His weariness, of appreciation
to His sleepless love. The gift it bestowed
was spent in a few minutes, but its influence
has travelled to heaven; Jesus imputed to it
the whole length of the way.

D O so with me also, O Lord! Put into
my box of ointment more than is
there! My box holds very little; but my
wish holds much; impute my wish to my
deed! The little I can do is lost in an hour.
The coin I gave the beggar is spent in
riotous living; the substance I shared with
the prodigal is squandered amid the swine.
But when I gave the coin, when I shared the
substance, I breathed a silent prayer too—a

wish of the heart. And the wish went beyond the poor gift, beyond the meagre coin; it asked for the beggar, it asked for the prodigal, a length of happy days. Put that wish into *my* alabaster box, O Christ! Impute to the mean offering not what it gives but what it would *fain* bestow! Impute to the material brass the spiritual gold! Count among the pieces of silver the coins that were only in my heart! Reckon amongst my charities the treasures I spent in *imagination* for Thy poor —the treasures I *would* have spent had they been mine! Put down to my credit not what I gave, but what I willed to give! Then shalt Thou say of me, as Thou saidst of Mary. 'Thou hast wrought a good work in me.'

CHAPTER XIV

THE COSMOPOLITAN CONSCIOUSNESS OF JESUS

JESUS rested overnight at Bethany—probably in that hallowed home where He had received the anointing. In the morning, instead of returning to His retreat, He proceeded towards Jerusalem. And as He drew near Jerusalem there awaited Him a surprise. It was close upon the time of the Passover, and the metropolis was being filled from all quarters. But it seemed as if the Passover itself had become of secondary interest. Instead of saying, 'The Feast is drawing near,' men said, 'Jesus is drawing near.' As the report of His proximity spread it was felt that He would come to the Passover. The expectation created a ferment. Crowds began to gather and grow as the hours advanced. At last, when He appeared, the excitement rose

to fever heat. He was surrounded by an
enthusiastic multitude, mad with admiration.
Behind, before, on either side, a mighty crowd
surged and waved and undulated, shouting,
applauding, rejoicing. Each vied with the
other in his expression of loyalty. Some
cried 'Hosannah!'; some apostrophised Him
as the coming King; some cut down the
neighbouring palm branches to make a carpet
for His feet; some went further still, and
spread their garments in the way that He
might walk on them. Perhaps never since
the building of the Second Temple had
so many hearts in Israel felt such a thrill
of joy.

I have said it took Jesus by surprise. By
this I mean to indicate that He did not *plan*
the demonstration. If I had only the first
three gospels to guide me I should think
that He *did*; for these place in the fore-
ground His preparing to ride into Jerusalem
in an attitude of majesty. But St. John
corrects the impression, and shows that the
riding was suggested by the enthusiasm, not

the enthusiasm by the riding.   What *reason*
had Jesus to anticipate such a reception—
to prepare for it beforehand!   The last time
He had met that multitude it had been actuated by equal enthusiasm—but on the other
side; they who now shouted 'Hosannah!'
had a few weeks before cried, 'Stone him!'
When Jesus had on that occasion withdrawn
from Jerusalem He had withdrawn from a
storm and on account of that storm.   He
was afraid for His disciples—afraid lest the
few remaining flowers which He could still
present to His Father might be withered.
Even after the Lazarus episode He had not
gone back to Jerusalem; He had resumed
His life of seclusion.   His present breaking
with that life had not been through the
anticipation of any triumphal entry; it had
been simply to attend a social gathering
which had the nature of a thanksgiving.
When He was anointed at Bethany what
He felt was not triumph; it was rather a
support against sinking.   The thought of His
burial was still uppermost.   It had not

occurred to Him to view the Lazarus episode
as the Jewish multitude viewed it—in the
light of a trophy. What one does for the
glory of the Father is never looked upon as
a source of fame. I have no hesitation in
saying that when Jesus on this occasion went
up to Jerusalem He had no intention of entering the city in any other way than that of
a private individual. The plaudits of the
crowd surprised Him.

'But,' you say, 'Jesus *yielded* to these
plaudits; He allowed Himself to be carried
down with the stream; does not that seem
an incongruous attitude under the imminent
shadow of death?' Incongruous? Is it
incongruous under the shadow of death to
dream of a kingdom that will embrace all
nations? Have we not said that things are
widest in the valley? Have we not seen
that the nearer we come to the foot of the
ladder the nearer we draw to those wants
which are common to all men? If so,
then the faith in a cosmopolitan kingdom
should be *deepest* under the shadow of death.

Remember, *Christ's* was a cosmopolitan king-dom. His was not the hope of a national sovereignty ; it was the hope of a sovereignty which should destroy the distinction of nations in the brotherhood of all men. What time could be more appropriate for the proclama-tion of such a kingdom than the presence of that shadow which eventually covers all!

But there was also a *historical* appropriate-ness in this yielding of Jesus to the hour of theocratic triumph. Remember, He had just come from the vicinity of the Jewish wilderness —the old wilderness of His temptations. Did He recall these temptations—the order of them, the truth that lay beneath them? Let *us* try to recall them. You remember how three panoramic views passed in turn before Him. The tempter said successively, 'Be a prophet,' 'Be a king,' 'Be a priest.' He said, first, 'Be a prophet; manifest your glory by heading a democratic movement for the better sustenance of the people;[1] make the stones

[1] The 'prophet' among the Jews *represented* the democratic movement.

bread.' He said, secondly, 'Be a king; manifest your glory by a temporal dominion; rule
among the nations.' He said, thirdly, 'Be a
priest; manifest your glory by an act of
sacrifice; cast yourself down from the pinnacle
of the temple.'

And Jesus had said to Himself: 'I will do
none of these things with such a motive. Not
for my *own* glory will I be either prophet,
king, or priest; but I will be each in turn for
the glory of my Father.' Hitherto He had
been mainly the prophet—the redresser of the
people's wrongs. His Galilean ministry had
been chiefly democratic—for the good of the
toiling masses; He had been feeding the
multitude with bread in the wilderness. In
one sense it was a local ministry, for the
wrongs of that multitude were wrongs in-
digenous to a particular soil. But, as the Son
of Man descended into the vale, the local had
given place to the cosmopolitan; the vision of
the universal *king* had gradually been super-
seding that of the Galilean *prophet*. And now
as He stood under the shadow of death there

floated before His gaze the shadow of His coming Empire—an Empire which, like death, should enfold within its embrace all ranks and conditions of men. It was this which made Him yield to the solicitation of the hour of triumph. It was this which impelled Him to ride majestically into Jerusalem. It was this which induced Him to refuse the request of the Pharisees, ' Master, rebuke Thy disciples ! ' He wanted them to see Him in a new relation, in a wider relation. He wanted them to associate the cosmopolitan sweep of His kingdom rather with *this* hour than with any other, to behold in the fact of the cross the promise and power of the crown.

Now, it is a very remarkable circumstance that from this time forward the words of Jesus become the words of a cosmopolitan sovereign. They get a new ring—a ring of world-empire. That tone abides with them on to the end; even the hour of sacrifice does not change it. Nowhere does Jesus address so wide an audience as in this time of seeming limitation; nowhere does He aim so high as when on the steps of the cross. It is no longer the Pharisees and the Sadducees that are the theme of His contemplation; it is the united nations of the world. Jerusalem has dwindled into a point; Judea has contracted into a single room in the house of the Father. Before the eye of Jesus there flashes a new vision of judgment —the judgment of *nations*. He sees the kingdoms of the world divided as the sheep and the goats are divided, some are on the right hand, others on the left. And the principle which is to decide their position is the amount of their *charity*. The humanitarian nations are to be in front, in the van—those who fed the hungry, healed the sick, reformed the prisoner. The non-humanitarian nations are to be in the rear—those who oppressed the poor and had nothing for the criminal but a chain. That is what I understand Him to mean when He cries, ' Now is the judgment of *this* world'—the judgment that does not need to wait for *another* world. Has not the verdict been confirmed by secular history? Are not the humanitarian nations the progressive nations? do they not sit at the right hand of power? Are not the non-humanitarian nations the backward nations? are they not left behind in the march of Man? Truly there was human wisdom in this Divine vision!

It was because in Jerusalem Jesus saw the *want* of this universal humanity that as He drew near He wept over it. Twice. only twice, do I read of the tears of Jesus—at the grave of Bethany and at the entrance to Jerusalem. Both were cosmopolitan weepings. In each case the cause of mourning was the same—because Man had not realised his full human destiny. At the grave of Bethany He wept because the human soul had failed to apprehend its immortality; at the gates of Jerusalem He wept because the human soul had failed to reach the idea of perfect brother-hood. This idea of perfect brotherhood was the thing which Jerusalem required for her peace, and for want of which she was stranded. She had missed her destiny among the nations by thinking too much of her nationality.

And was it not this same moral which Jesus

meant to point when in the streets of that
Jerusalem He met, the next day, with a
deputation from another land? It was a band
of Greeks who had come up to the Passover
and who desired to see Jesus. In one sense
the Greek was like the Jew—he was self-con-
tained. The Greek valued his culture on the
same ground that the Jew valued his religion,
because it distinguished him from other men.
Therefore to him also Jesus pointed the moral
of self-forgetfulness, 'Except a corn of wheat
fall into the ground and die, it abideth alone.'
It is as if He had said: 'If you want to be a
great nation, diffuse your light. Do not seek
to keep your privileges to yourself. Throw
them over the wall; spread them broadcast.
You are, after all, only a section of a larger
life—humanity. Whatever you have, you hold
in trust for the race. Be true to your steward-
ship; be true to your universal mission. You
will stand at the right hand among the nations
when you realise that your culture is for the
service of Man.'

And when we reach that marvellous discourse of Jesus reported in St. Matthew xxiv., wherein He casts a prophetic eye over the page of unwritten history, what do we find? I do not ask you to expound that passage; I do not offer you any exposition of it; I leave that to the commentators. But, whatever be the reading of the mystery, one thing at least is clear—and that is the central thing. Jesus meant to say that there would never be peace among the nations of the world until the sign of the Son of Man appeared in heaven. There would be no rest until then. Until then the sun would be darkened and the moon would refuse her light and the stars would fall from the sky and the powers of the firmament would be shaken. There would be wars and rumours of war; there would be famine and pestilence and earthquake in many lands. But when the sign of the Son of Man should arise in heaven there would be a great calm; a voice would say to the nations, ' Peace, be still! '

What was this sign of the Son of Man in heaven? It was the cross in high places—the spirit of unselfishness among the great nations. Heaven is the prophetic symbol for majesty; the 'sign of Christ' is the cross of sacrifice. To see Christ's sign in heaven was to behold humanitarianism in the centres of power. That vision had never yet been seen—not in Judea, not in Babylon, not in Egypt, not in Syria, not in Rome. In no land, however free, had Man yet been recognised as man. Nowhere had the corn of wheat fallen into the ground and died. Nowhere had a nation realised that its pride was a thing to be crucified. Nowhere had an empire wakened to the conviction that it was a servant for the common weal. And Jesus said that without such a waking there could be nothing but national tribulations— nothing but darkenings of the sun, nothing but rumours of the storm. There was needed by each citizen a cosmopolitan consciousness— the sign of the Son of Man.

Let me resume the narrative. Jesus by His triumphal entry into Jerusalem played into the hands of His enemies. He gave what Caiaphas waited for — a pretext for arrest.

That pretext could only be found in an insult
to Rome. Hitherto nothing had been done
by Jesus which could have been construed as
anti-Roman; it had been all anti-Jewish. But
now Caiaphas might cry, 'The Lord hath
delivered him into our hands!' Was not this
triumphal entry all that was wanted to serve
the purpose of the Sanhedrin! Had they not
now a definite ground for arresting Jesus in
the interest of the empire! Could they not
make this incident tell against him in the eyes
of Rome! Why not represent this as an act
of revolution! Had he not headed a tumul-
tuous band uttering treasonable cries—cries
that impugned the supremacy of Cæsar!
Had he not shaken the allegiance of the
people to imperial authority! Had he not
exhibited a spectacle which on that undis-
ciplined rabble must have the effect of inciting
to rebellion! Surely the legal pretext had at
last been found for laying their hands on the
Galilean!

Yes, the pretext—but not the opportunity.
How could they arrest Him without that

Roman interposition which they did not want? He was for the moment surrounded by the multitude; they were hot for Him, they would fight for Him.   True, it was only for the moment; their fervour would pass away.   But so would the legal opportunity; Rome would not be influenced by a danger in the past.   It was an awkward situation.   They were saved by an act of treachery in the camp of Jesus— an act perpetrated by a member of that first league of pity which had hitherto clung to Him through every change of fortune.   I will not tarnish the picture of the multitude's enthusiasm by introducing the miscreant here.

STILL make Thine entrance into our cities, O Lord!   Our cities need Thee yet. There is much in our Jerusalems that might well draw Thy tears.   Every good citizen cries for 'Him that cometh in the name of the Lord.'   The members of our crafts and guilds are not adequate to their work until they see *Thee* in the gate.   Our young men are unworthy of their youth until they see *Thee* in the gate. Our women fall beneath their sex until they see *Thee* in the gate. Our mothers have no ideal for their children until they see *Thee* in the gate. Our children have no glory in their picture-book until they see *Thee* in the gate. Stand in the gate, O Christ! Stand till the crowds gather; stand till the toilers gaze; stand till through our streets we make for Thee a way! Our cities shall flourish like the palm-tree when the branches of the palm shall be strewn for *Thee.*

CHAPTER XV

JUDAS

SCARCELY had the echoes of the multitude died away when there stood at the door of the high priest an unwonted visitor. His name was Judas Iscariot. He was one of the innermost circle of the Galilean band. He was not only a member of the original league; he was treasurer of the company's funds. It was a post requiring some culture and more shrewdness; and it was doubtless these qualities that had commended him for the situation.

What is it that brings this man to the door of the high priest? Has he come with overtures from Jesus? Has he brought from his Master a proposal of alliance with the Sanhedrin? I can imagine such a hope to have flashed through the heart of Caiaphas. I am sure he would have welcomed such a sugges-

tion. A Christ who would support the kingdom of the theocracy instead of the kingdom of God would have been to him a
valuable ally. But in his wildest dreams
Caiaphas had never hoped for what he was
about to receive. Judas stands before him
and says: 'I am come to extricate you from
all your difficulties. You wish to secure the
person of the Galilean without foreign aid,
without domestic bloodshed. You may; you
can. I have the power to give you what you
wish. I can point to the day and the hour
when you will find him unbefriended, alone.
What price will you put upon a service so
essential to your peace?'

Now, it is my opinion that Caiaphas would
have acceded to almost any sum. It was his
interest, however, to *minimise* the service.
The priesthood of Israel ought not to seem
afraid. He therefore makes light of the offer.
He determines in his own mind that he will
begin by proposing the lowest sum, and rise
in the scale in proportion to the demands of
Judas. Starting from the foot of the ladder

he offers at first the market price of a slave—
thirty pieces of silver. He must have laughed
inwardly when he offered it, and must have
waited to hear Judas laugh outwardly. To
his astonishment, to the astonishment of all
posterity, the outward laugh was never uttered.
Judas never makes a demur, never suggests
that his possession is worth more. He seems
quite oblivious of the value of what he offers.
He proposes no rise in his demand. He
plants his foot upon the lowest round and
holds it there; he accepts the contemptible
sum—thirty pieces of silver!

Yet Judas was a covetous man. If ever a
man knew the value of money, Judas knew it.
He had been for some time suspected of com-
mercial dishonesty. The love of gold had
been too strong for him. It had led him into
nefarious transactions. One of his brethren in
the league, in plain language, calls him ' a thief,'
and suggests that he appropriated the dona-
tions to the poor. Yet this is the man who,
in exchange for the most valuable information
—information whose value he had thoroughly

estimated, accepted without murmur the market price of a slave!

This fact has led me to two conclusions— first, however covetous Judas may have been, covetousness was not his motive for the betrayal of Jesus; and, second, he wished it to be *thought* that covetousness *was* his motive. If you come to my conclusion on the first point you will have no difficulty in appreciating the second. We have to consider, first, the *real* motive for the betrayal, and then, why Judas pretended to act from a *different* motive.

Judas never sold his Lord with the view of obtaining thirty pieces of silver. The very badness of the man prevents such a supposition; it is inconsistent with his past avarice. The acceptance of so small a sum is conclusive to my mind that money was not in the question. I believe the mind of Judas to have been at this time animated by a *passion*; this alone suits our Lord's description, 'I have chosen you twelve, and one of you is subject to diabolic influences.' A diabolic or demoniacal influence was a *passion*. It was

something which swept over the mind in gusts,
which operated drastically, which took captive
the will. Avarice is not such a state. It is
not a passion ; it is rather the want of passion.
It does not come in gusts; it is a permanent
state of the heart existing equally at all times.
I am not denying that avarice was a quality of
Judas. What I maintain is that he must have
had another bad quality of a different kind, of
a more violent and intermittent kind. Everything about the narrative shows that the
motive which led him to the betrayal was one
which took possession of his mind periodically,
almost spasmodically. It came to him at
certain times and in certain places. It was
not an atmosphere which permeated all his
actions as his avarice did. Rather did it
come to him in special currents and break
upon him in peculiar storms.[1] The thirty
pieces of silver will *not* explain the deed of
Judas.

What, then, does explain it? We have seen

[1] The language of St. John xiii. 27 seems to bear out this
view.

that it came from a passion—a passion that took the form of a Satanic impulse, a passion which arose at periodic intervals, and which in the moment of its coming overmastered the will, and possessed the heart. Is there a passion in the human soul that will correspond to these conditions? I know of only one—jealousy. It is the root of malice and hatred and envy and all uncharitableness. The passion of drink has wrought many evils; but they have not been the result of deliberation. The passion of anger has kindled deadly fires; but we never associate it with that which is mean or malign. But jealousy is a lurid power, an underground power. It works in the mine; it *under*mines. It is a subterranean fire that can burn invisibly, stealthily. It feeds upon its own flame. Anger exhausts itself by its very exercise; jealousy is quickened by the spending of its gall!

Now, I believe this to have been the passion of Judas. I think his jealousy was deeper than his avarice—it was, I think, the *root* of his avarice. What I conceive him to have

said to his own heart is something like this:
'I feel that my merits in this community have
not been properly recognised. I have done
more physical work than any man of the
league; I have gathered and disbursed the
material funds of the company. But my work
has been disparaged because it *is* physical.
Men without half my talent are set above me
because they are said to possess a vapoury
thing called spirituality. Peter is looked up
to as a ringleader. James and John are called
pillars. Philip and Andrew get the honour
of introducing the Greeks. But I am left
among the inferiors of the band—I, who am
equal to the best of them! My work, for-
sooth, is only physical; it does not entitle me
to be taken up to the mount with the pillar
brothers. I should like to show the league
what they would be *without* the physical. They
look down upon mere financial talent; where
would they *be* without finance! If I were to
become the rich man of the company, I might
teach them not to depreciate the gift of finding
gold. I should then pass from the rear to

the van. I should make this proud upper
circle feel their dependence on me for bread;
the men of the mount would find that they
had to seek their subsistence from the man
on the plain!'

Such is my analysis of the mind of Judas.
I believe the spirit of jealousy was the great
incentive to the spirit of avarice. I do not
think that originally his discontent extended
to the *Master*. He must have often heard
Jesus rebuke the ambition of His disciples,
and it must have been balm to him. His
first design was to outshine the upper circle.
He strove to gain that end by getting rich.
His mode of getting rich was the purloining
of the missionary funds. By and by, dark
suspicions arose; at last, one day, detection
came. And *then* in no measured terms must
have fallen the rebuke of the Master; and
Judas himself must have seen that within the
circle of that band his must be for ever only
a servant's place.

This Judas could not brook. Before he
would consent to take, in the band, the position

of a permanent subordinate he resolved to break up the band altogether. I believe this was his real motive. There are some mean natures who would rather see a thing destroyed than have another get it instead of them. Judas was one of these. He sought the arrest of Jesus as the only available means of breaking up the league of pity. The death of Jesus, the personal suffering of Jesus, was no part of his programme; his object in smiting the shepherd was that the *sheep* might be scattered. He was actuated by jealousy. He saw a boat sailing over a very pleasant sea, and he was himself forbidden to enter it. He resolved that since he was forbidden nobody else should enter it — that he would forthwith sink it. That was his motive—a dastardly motive, a contemptibly mean motive, yet a motive in its nature radically distinct from the actual avarice for gold.

But now, if Judas was to receive any future favour from the priesthood, it was essential that this motive should be *concealed*. It was no compliment to that body that a man should

say, 'I reject the service of Jesus, because I
have been refused promotion in it.' That was
practically to state that he was still in principle an adherent of that hated sect which had
been founded by the Galilean. A man with
the business talents of Judas might expect *promotion* in a worldly sphere like that of the
Jewish theocracy. It would be shutting the
door upon himself to say that he had not
really returned to a conviction of the national
faith, but had only yielded to the expediency
of the hour. Judas felt that it would be better
to assume another motive—a motive which
should indicate a change of Christian conviction.
Jealousy did not indicate a change of conviction; it rather suggested that the longing
for the old cause still was there. But avarice,
the sordid love of gold, the greed of personal
gain—this was a motive which would at once
relieve a man from the charge of sympathy
with Jesus! Judas said: 'I will dissimulate.
I will represent a cause for my deed, different
from the real one. I will suggest to the chief
priests a motive which they, of all men, will

appreciate—the love of gold. Are not the men in high places often guilty of selling the truth for a bribe? These will best understand me, will most kindly remember me, if I put a price upon my service.'

That the motive of Judas was jealousy is to my mind made clear by one passage, St. Luke xxii. 21-24. Jesus is there telling His disciples of the man who would betray Him. Suddenly He turns round and points a moral to the disciples themselves (verse 25 and *seq.*). And the reason of the transition is explained by the evangelist in verse 24 : 'there was also a strife among *them* who should be the greatest.' If you so emphasise the word 'them' you will get a flood of meaning on the passage. Will it not read thus?—'Do not think *you* are altogether exempt from the danger of the pit into which this man will fall! He has simply carried to an exaggerated height a sin which is present in you all—a sin whose development I have watched with deep concern. Beware of jealousy! it is the sin of him who shall betray me. You have the germ of the same complaint ;

stifle it, suppress it, kill it ! If you suffer it to
grow, there are no bounds to its possibilities;
it may stretch between you and the sun, and
eclipse the light of heaven !'

The betrayal by Judas is, indeed, to all of us
a very solemn incident. It shows us that no
religious *environment* will suffice to make a
man religious. The environment of Judas was
perfect. Side by side with Jesus from the
beginning, auditor of all His words, witnesser
of all His deeds, recipient even of His personal
ordination to the service of humanity, this man
had everything given to him which *could* be
given from the *outside*. He had more oppor-
tunities of being with Jesus than any of the
others. His office of treasurer to the company
was one which involved frequent interviews
with the Master. Never was a man so privileged ; never was a life placed in an environment so Divine! And yet, Judas did not
become a religious man. His life destroyed
his environment as the worm destroyed Jonah's
gourd. I do not believe that at the outset
he was altogether free from the promise and

potency of Divine grace; I do not believe Jesus
would have elected him to His ministry in the
absence of such a promise. But the worm got
in—the worm called jealousy. It gnawed
away the gourd. It vitiated the value of every
privilege. It made of none effect the Sermon
on the Mount; it destroyed the benefit of the
communion in the desert. Judas is the finest
existing testimony to the power of the internal.
He shows how powerless is everything else
unless supported from within. He is the
strongest comment on the passage, 'Keep thy
heart with all diligence, for out of *it* are the
issues of life.'

HOW shall I keep my heart from jealousy,
O Lord? Only by loving my brother
as myself. I can never be free from jealousy
by fleeing from the prize I covet. Often in my
hour of envy I have said to myself, 'Give up
the world, and you will have peace!' I forget
that the thing I covet is not the object in the
hand but the object in the fancy. In vain I

summon the wings of a dove and flee away; I carry in my *heart* the glitter of my brother's gold! Not by the wings of a dove shall I find rest, O Lord; only by the wings of Thy spirit —love's wings! Not even by depreciating the prize shall I find rest! Thou wouldst not have me cease to admire its beauty; Thou wouldst have me rejoice that its beauty is in the possession of my *brother*. I need, not less glitter, but more love. I should not like to reach peace by disparaging my brother's possession—by saying, 'It is not pretty.' Nay, rather, for his sake, would I *revel* in its loveliness, would I admire it more and more. I would feel that my brother is a part of myself; I would rejoice in his pleasure as a pleasure of my own. If he is taken up to the mount and I am left on the plain, I would not solace myself by saying, 'The mount is cold.' I would say, 'I thank Thee, O Lord, that a member of my body has been invigorated by a stream of Thy glory.' So shall I lose the jealousy and still preserve the joy!

CHAPTER XVI

THE OPENING OF THE SECOND COMMUNION

WE are now approaching that scene, or rather, that succession of scenes in the great gallery which I call the second communion. The first communion was the feeding of the multitude in the desert. In the former part of this book I suggested a contrast between these two epochs in the life of Jesus. The first was essentially a secular communion—the giving of physical bread; the second was to be distinctively a spiritual fellowship—a breaking of the bread of life. The first was a descent of Jesus to the multitude; the second was to be a drawing of the multitude up to Jesus. The first was initiated by the want of the *crowd.* But the second was to have its beginning in a hunger of the soul of *Jesus*: 'Earnestly have I desired to eat this Passover with you before I suffer.' He remembers the anointing at Bethany. He remembers what strength it brought Him. He remembers how the communion of one human heart had braced Him for His burial. Would not the effect be repeated by the communion of *twelve* human hearts representative of twelve times twelve thousand? The desire of Jesus was a desire for personal stimulus. I do not think it was the wish to say farewell. I do not think He ever looked upon the Last Supper as a farewell. The consciousness on His part was *not* that of impending separation. He did not feel that He was bidding His disciples good-bye. He wished to meet them for a very different purpose. He wished, before entering that Gethsemane which death still held for Him, to gaze on the few gems which He had already won for His Father.

I have said that in the great gallery the picture of the second communion is not so much one scene as a succession of scenes. It seems to me to embrace four distinct stages. The first is the Passover — the communion with the Jewish past; it is the Feast prepared in the upper room of Jerusalem. The second is in the middle of that Feast; it is the communion of the Lord's Supper, where that same upper room becomes transfigured into the guest-chamber in which Christ receives His disciples. The third is in the garden of Gethsemane; it is the sighing of the heart of Jesus for those who are *not* disciples, His longing to find a place in the soul of the sinner. The fourth is the cross of Calvary; it is the communion with future ages — the sure and unbroken confidence that the death from which He shrank in Gethsemane would become His highest glory, 'I, if I be lifted up from the earth, will draw all men unto me.' We shall see, as we proceed, how these fold into one another.

And first. Almost at that same moment when Judas was betraying Jesus to the Jewish theocracy, Jesus was cherishing for that theocracy a sentiment of friendship. He was preparing to keep the Feast—the national Passover Feast. He had no need to keep it. He pro-

fessed to have, personally, transcended it. He
would have said to all such gatherings, 'I have
meat to eat that ye know not of; my meat is
to do the will of Him that sent me, and to
finish His work.' No Passover Feast had
'finished the work' for the Father. The killing
of the Pascal lamb had expiated nothing,
atoned for nothing. No priest pretended it
had done so, or intended it should do so;
it was but a type of what the nation felt was
due to God from Man. Jesus had designed
to be the anti-type; He had been offering His
life *in the place of* the Passover lamb. To
keep the Feast was for Him a work of super-
erogation. It was like entering a dark room
and lighting a candle to peruse a document
which could be read in broad daylight. Yet
Jesus submitted to go back—back in the order
of development. As in the days of His own
baptism, He lit the candle when He had the
sunlight. He resolved to keep the Feast of
His fathers because it *was* the Feast of His
fathers. It is a grand testimony to His dis-
like of all bereavements! This Feast was a

poor, imperfect thing ; yet, for His love of the past, He would not let it go. He would raise it as He raised Lazarus. He would revivify it with His own presence. He would give it a new significance which should make it a glory for ever.

And He did. In that upper room where He kept the Passover with His disciples He showed each of them what a Paschal sacrifice should be. They had been quarrelling as to which should have the place nearest Himself. He taught them by a striking symbol that those nearest to Himself were the humblest in soul ; He took a towel and girded Himself, and washed their feet. The evangelist prefaces his account of the deed by these words, 'Knowing that He came from God and went to God.' And many a preacher reading the words has pointed the moral thus, 'Look how condescending Jesus was! although He knew He was so far above these poor creatures both in His origin and in His destiny, He yet stooped beneath His conscious position!' That is not my reading of the passage, nor my

moral from it.   Where, think you, lies the connection in the thought of Jesus between wash-
ing the disciples' feet and remembering that
He came from God and went to God?   Is it
not clearly this?—' My course has been humility
all through—from beginning to end.   When I
came from God I came *down* ; my mission was
to surrender my own will.   When I *go* to God
I shall pass to Him through depths lower still
—through the valley of the shadow of death.
This act of service towards you is to me in
keeping with all that is gone before and with
all that is to follow.'   The clause is meant to
exclude the idea of condescension, to show how
thorough was the surrender of the true Paschal
Lamb.   The lamb of the Passover was offered
only once a year ; but the surrender of the will
of Jesus had been made each morn and even.

All this took place at the *beginning* of the
meal ; the phrase in our version, 'supper being
ended,' is a very improbable reading.   Gradually, as the evening advanced, the meal
acquired a fresh meaning.   The associations of
the past seemed to fade from it.   Moment by

moment it lost its national character; it became a banquet for the hour. Its interest
began to centre in a single life. One form
took precedence of all history, one figure
towered over all time; it was that of the Man
of Galilee! There was no change in the environment. It was the same room, the same
furniture, the same provision for the Feast.
Yet to the eye of these disciples it seemed as if
the Passover had passed away, and as if they
were sitting at a new Feast—the Feast of the
Lord Jesus!

By-and-by Judas quits the party. He had
probably in the course of conversation learned
the purpose of Jesus to spend that evening in
the Garden of Gethsemane; at all events he
knows the fact, and he goes to reveal it. And
then it would seem as if an incubus were
lifted from the soul of Jesus. He, too, feels as
if all things were made new. From the fragments of that Passover supper He inaugur-
ates another feast—a feast which He boldly
affirms will be observed periodically to the
end of the world, and which through all the

centuries will be the sign of union with His
name. With striking originality He declares
that it is to stand for ages in memory of Himself, nay, in memory of that in Him which had
seemed most like disaster and defeat—His
sacrifice of expiation. As a symbol of that
sacrifice, He breaks a piece of bread and pours
wine into a cup ; 'This bread,' He cries, 'is my
body which is being broken for you ; this cup
is my blood which is being shed for you.'

You will observe how I have emphasised the
present tense—'*being* broken,' '*being* shed.'
That is the sense of the original. It is often
explained by saying that the vividness to Jesus
of the image of coming death made it already
to Him a present reality. That is not my
view—that is not the view of this book. To
my mind, Jesus speaks in the present because
His expiation was in the present. He was not
waiting for death, to begin His work. Nay,
previous to Gethsemane, death was the only
thing which was dark to Him, the only drop of
the cup which was mysterious in His sight,
and which, if possible, He would fain have had

remitted. The mystery of death to Jesus was not in the cloud overhanging the future life—He had no such cloud ; it lay in a cloud which overhung His own work for His Father, and which seemed to endanger it. His work for His Father had been going on since morning. From dawn to dark He had been surrendering Himself to His Father, yielding up flesh and blood by a sacrifice of the will. From dawn to dark He had been giving His life to God, seeking to atone for a world's lovelessness. From the moment He took the servant's form He had begun to shed His blood, to pour out His life in the work of His Father. The Lord's Supper was to the men who first partook of it associated mainly with the broken *life* of Jesus. It got a wider significance by-and-by. Within a few years a Paul could say, ' As often as you eat this bread you show the Lord's *death*.' But by that time Gethsemane was *past*. The clouds had rolled away from the Garden, and the final act of the tragedy had appeared—as the brightest of all the flowers. As yet, we have not entered the Garden. We are still

before the gate. We must not expect at the
entrance the light which is only at the end.
Jesus gave to His disciples the bread and the
cup He had *already* taken—no less, no more.
He looked forward to the future for a *fuller*
communion, ' I shall drink it *anew* with you in
my Father's kingdom.'

And now the supper is ended, and they sing
a parting hymn. Sometimes after the close
of a service we linger and converse for a few
minutes in the place of its celebration. So
was it here. Between the final song of praise
and the going out into the night Jesus speaks
those words of comfort which are embodied in
the fourteenth chapter of St. John's Gospel.
This, at least, is my opinion, and the opening
words seem to bear it out. Is not this what
they say: ' I have lately been preparing for
you an upper room of communion; but now
you are compelled to leave it. Such joys on
earth are ever fleeting. But let not your heart
be troubled! I am about to prepare for you
another upper room where you shall be with
me again in *permanent* communion. In my

Father's house are many rooms—not fleeting, as here, but abiding for ever. I go to furnish one of these for you, that the communion begun here may be perpetuated yonder.'   He adds : 'If it were not so, I would have told you.   I would have made this a farewell.   I would not have asked you to keep a feast in remembrance of me if I did not know that I should be alive. But I *shall* be alive, nay, I shall manifest my life.   My Spirit shall be with you.   I shall be invisibly present with you—to guide you into all truth, especially to keep you from all fear. I will send you my peace, which is quite different from the world's peace.   The world can only give its peace by causing the cloud to pass ; mine can come in the *presence* of the cloud.'

Jesus was, indeed, conscious at this moment of a twofold experience—a simultaneous peace and pain. Perhaps it would be more correct to say that He had at the same moment a personal peace and an impersonal pain.   It was all right with Himself, all right with that chaplet of flowers which He had *already* gathered for His Father.   He had perfect con-

fidence in the preservation of those whom the
Father had already given Him—and this in
the full foresight that for a time they would
desert Him. But there was a *pain* simultaneous
with the peace—a pain for those whom the
Father had *not* yet given Him—a pain for that
world which hated both Him and His Father.
It was a grand thing that for the moment He
could subordinate the pain to the peace—that
for the sake of comforting others, He could
bury for an hour that grief which, though
impersonal, was all His own.

Suddenly He cries, ' Arise, let us go hence ! '
They issue forth from the upper room into the
moonlit night. They pass through the streets
of Jerusalem. They descend to the valley of
Kidron ; they rise again by the western slope
of the Mount of Olives. They are bound for
the Oilpress Garden—Gethsemane's Garden.
Ever and anon they halt by the way, and at
each pause Jesus pours Himself forth in words
not of gloom but of cheer—those words which
have been known as His ' Farewell Sermon.'
I should say there is no note so *foreign* to

them as that of farewell. Their refrain is the reverse—'Abide in me! Cling to me! Never let me go!' There is, indeed, *one* note of finality, 'I have glorified Thee on the earth; I have finished the *work* that Thou gavest me to do!' Jesus feels that the active part of His day is ended, that the night is coming when no man can work. Whatever future service lay before Him could not be active service. There is a deep significance in the words, 'I have glorified *Thee*; and now, O Father, glorify *me*!' It is as if He had said: 'I must henceforth be *passive* in Thy hand. No more can I work miracles for *Thee*; Thou must work Thy miracles for *me*. My time for action is past; my time for bearing is come. Hitherto I have been *labouring* for Thee; I must now be heavy-laden for Thee. I cannot any longer minister to *Thy glory*; minister to *my need*, O my Father!'

That is to my mind the only note of pain in all the song. I am glad that it is there. It shows me, better than anything else, what the peace of Jesus was; it reveals to me, as nothing

else could reveal, the difference of that peace
from the peace of the world. It unveils to me
the fact that the peace of Jesus is a peace
contemporaneous with pain. It tells me that
His attitude of mind at this time was a voluntary effort, an unselfish effort. It was a determination to keep His eye on the bright side
of the picture in order that the companions of
His early ministry might see no shadow of a
latent pain.

LET *me* walk with Thee, O Lord, on the
way from that upper room ; let *me*
enter into Thine unselfish spirit ! If I have a
troubled corner in my heart, and those beside
me have a troubled corner too, help me to look
to the side that is *not* troubled ! Let me *cover*
the dark place in my heart while my sad
friends are with me ! I can *un*cover it when
I reach Gethsemane—when I shall be alone
with my grief. But here in the public walk,
here in the streets of Jerusalem, here in the
meeting with men bearing their own sadness,

let me keep mine eye on what I hold of *bright-ness*! Let me meet my weeping brother on the *sunny* side of my way! Let me refuse to look at *my Gethsemane* until I have led him through *his Jerusalem*! Let me conceal the place of my pain till he has gazed on the spot of my peace! So shall I be Thy disciple; so shall I walk with Thee from the upper room!

CHAPTER XVII

GETHSEMANE

I AM now come to the suppressed hour of Jesus. I can use no other expression. I do not regard the grief of the Garden as a sudden thing; rather does it seem to me a thing long repressed. From the memorable day in which He is recorded to have 'rejoiced in spirit' there had come to Jesus no moment of unclouded joy. His hours of brightness had been purchased by keeping His eye exclusively in one direction and ignoring the dark sides which were none the less felt to be there. Even His walk from Jerusalem to the Mount of Olives is a peace in the midst of pain; and the intercessory prayer with which it closes, rising as it does to heights of triumph, contains, as we have seen, the transition to Gethsemane.

With the entrance into the Garden the long-repressed hour at last struck. The sorrow which Jesus had kept under lock and key at length broke forth and filled the air with its presence. He had said, 'I have finished the work which Thou gavest me to do.' It is when work is *done* that the sorrows of the soul assert themselves. Griefs which lie latent in the time of action resume their sway when the hands are folded. The sense of a lost occupation, the feeling that we have nothing more to do, is ever the occasion when the troubles of the heart emerge from their hiding-place. This utterance of Jesus, in itself an expression of grateful gladness, is perhaps the very key which opens the gate into His garden of pain.

Not in equal degrees did Jesus admit His disciples to a vision of His grief. He allowed them all to enter the Garden; but he took three apart from the rest — the same three who had witnessed His transfigured glory — Peter, James, and John. Not even these had a perfect view; He stood somewhat apart from them also. Perhaps we of modern times have a nearer view than any of these. We have brought to our perception of the Portrait an experience of nearly nineteen Christian centuries. Ours is not physically a front view; but on that very account we may have superior advantages for being spectators in the great gallery. The mind of the Master is more on a level with *our* experience than with that of the men who watched with Him in the Garden. These were miles below Him. They did not then understand Him. We understand Him now better than they did that night; we, and not they, should be the observers in the Garden. Let *us* watch with Him in this hour! Let *us* take our stand beside the lonely Sufferer! We do not need to return to a past age; He was then living in our *present* experience; He was in advance of His time. Let us view the shadows of His night by the light we have derived from Him!

Let us look first at the form in which His sorrow expressed itself. The forms even of the same grief are by no means *uni*form.

There are, I think, three different ways in which the same form of suffering may express itself, and in each of which the pain may have equal intensity. There are some whose sorrow takes the form of numbness; their spirit of infirmity becomes a dumb spirit; they present to the bystander the attitude of stony apathy. There are some whose sorrow takes the form of rebellion; they rail against the system of the universe; they impugn the justice of Almighty God. And there are some whose sorrow takes the form of effusiveness; they pour forth the torrent of their grief. They do not let it drown their senses like the first class; they do not divert it into anger like the second; they give it outward play, they dwell on itself alone.

Now, this third is the form taken by the grief of Jesus. He gives it full play. He makes no effort to hide it from His *followers*, for the simple reason that He is not ashamed of it before His *Father*. There is no rebellion in it, no questioning of the goodness of the

Father; there is simply an abandonment to the sense of pain such as one sees exhibited by a little child in suffering, 'My soul is exceeding sorrowful, even unto death,' 'Tarry ye here while I go and pray yonder.' We see the spectacle of a soul 'in agony'; and the agony finds visible expression in sweat that falls to the ground like drops of blood; while His cry for help rings through the Garden, 'Father, if it be possible, let this cup pass from me!'

What was the cup against which Jesus prayed? The word 'this' seems to me significant. It is an antithesis to that other cup which He had given to His disciples at the Last Supper. He had no dubiety about *that* cup; He would not have given it to His disciples had He felt dubiety. Up to that point His course as the expiation for the sin of the world had been clear. It must, therefore, have become dark *since* then. We are driven to seek a solution within narrow limits —the limits of the Garden. Whatever this cup was which Jesus wanted to pass from

Him, one thing at least is certain—it was in some way connected with the prospect of His *death*.

But in what way? That is the question which now opens upon us. It will not do to throw a veil of absolute mystery over the scene. He has asked us to 'watch' with Him. Watching implies sympathy, and sympathy demands participation. A grief which is to us an absolute mystery cannot be a ground of sympathy. 'Could ye not watch with me one hour?' asks Jesus in the Garden. Our ability to do so must be proportionate to our understanding of the nature of His sorrow. That is true of every sick-nurse; the secret of her watching is her sympathy, and the secret of her sympathy is her knowledge of the pain. If we would share in the vigil, we must attempt to draw aside the veil.

I repeat, then, the question—why did Jesus recoil from this particular moment? A great modern thinker has not scrupled to render His words 'My soul is exceeding sorrowful even unto death,' by the phrase, 'My soul is

exceeding sorrowful *to die.*' The suggestion
is that the Son of Man was recoiling, as you
and I would recoil, from death in the abstract
—shrinking humanly back from the shadows
that encompass the silent land.   Whatever
view I formed of the person of Jesus, it would
be impossible for me to entertain such a
thought.   Would it be consistent with the
Portrait, with any expression of the Portrait?
Here is a soul absolutely steeped in the
thought of immortality—a soul to whom the
other world has always been the real world
and *this* the land of shadows—a soul so confident of the life eternal that He speaks of it
as something which is begun on earth!   Here
is one who, according to the delineation of the
artist, has declared Himself to be already in
possession of this life eternal, who professes
to keep a reservoir of waters which will make
immortal the man who tastes of them!   According to that same Portrait He has just
proved the truth of His claim by a marvellous
and public exhibition of death's inability to
extinguish the spirit!   And yet, we are asked

to believe that immediately afterwards He pours out torrents of grief by reason of the fact that the valley of death which He is compelled to enter is too dark for His penetration, and that the shadow of death which He is compelled to meet is too deep for His piercing! Surely the statement of such an inconsistency is itself a refutation of it! Surely, theology apart, the canons of artistic interpretation would alone impel us to reject such a solution! The fear of death itself will not explain the grief of the Garden.

Nor is it explained by the anticipation of physical pain. Hundreds for the sake of Jesus have gone to the stake right joyously; hundreds through the heat of their love for Him have been oblivious of their *outward* fire. Is the disciple to be above his Lord! The martyrs in the cause of Jesus smile at the coming flame; and shall Jesus Himself *faint* because of it! Has He not Himself disparaged all physical suffering when weighed against mental advantage, 'Fear not them that kill the body and after that have nothing more that they *can* do!' It is not conceivable that Gethsemane could have owed its agony to the dread of physical pain. Nay, I am convinced that nothing personal could have caused the grief of Jesus, that it must have come from one source and one alone—the dread of an interference with His work of expiation. Is there anything to suggest such here?

Yes, there was ground for a *great* dread. His life had been revealing to the Father the possibilities of human righteousness. What of that awful *un*righteousness which His *death* would reveal! I conceive Him to have thus spoken with Himself: 'Is my labour to be all in vain! I have been trying to *compensate* the Father, trying to give Him a little joy in the world He has made. And now there is a storm coming which will sweep all my seeds away! The world is about to spurn my Father! The world is about to kill His chosen child! If I *am* the Messiah of the Father, nothing so bad has ever been done before. If I am the Messiah of the Father, then to kill *me* is to trample under foot the Father's joy.

Is my work for Him to be all undone!. I have laboured to make Him glad; I have planted for Him a flower in my heart; I have seen Him smile as He looked on it. And now the world would pluck the flower, would wither the flower! It would undo my work in a night —my work of reconciliation! It would decree the death of purity, the death of holiness, the death of justice, the death of mercy, the death of Love! How couldst Thou bear this, O my Father! Wouldst Thou not henceforth banish man from Thy soul! If it be possible, let this cup, the cup of *Thy* pain, pass from me!'

That is my reading of Christ's shrinking from His own death. He shrank, not from His cross, but from the world's share in it; *that* was the cup He wanted to pass from Him. He wanted it to pass in the interest of the world itself. He wanted to avert from that world the danger of wrecking His reconciling work. He wanted to save it from committing the blackest deed of sin ever perpetrated by the sons of men—a deed which He feared might fix for ever an impassable gulf between the life of the creature and the heart of the Father.

You will observe, all this sorrow of Jesus would have been impossible but for His consciousness of a unique moral purity. It is a singular thing that the hour of His utmost humiliation, the hour of His 'strong crying and tears,' is precisely that hour in which His consciousness of a supreme moral majesty blazes out most brightly. There have been men whose lives have oscillated between the day and the darkness—men who have felt their glory in the morning and their humiliation in the night. But that the hour of humiliation should itself be the result of conscious glory —that is a strange thing! It will only be found in one experience; it is a feature peculiar to the Portrait of Christ; it separates His from all other portraits. The grief of Gethsemane would have had no existence but for Christ's sense of holiness. Why does He deplore beyond everything else the world's state of mind in crucifying Him? Why does He look upon this prospect as the culmination of its sin?

Because it was a projected murder? Men had murdered before, crucified unjustly before. It was because this was a project to murder purity itself. Jesus was not simply an individual, did not at this hour view Himself in the light of an individual. He thought of Himself as an embodiment of sinlessness. The sting of death lay to Him in the fact that it was the world's effort to kill virtue, to obliterate goodness, to wipe out from the human heart the handwriting of the moral law.

'What a self-consciousness,' you say, 'on the part of Jesus!' The strange thing is that it is *not*—this is *another* exceptional feature of the Picture. A consciousness of being holy, there certainly is; but it is unaccompanied by any egotism, any sense of self-importance. When we are impeded in our breathing, we become *conscious* of our breathing, and we realise its value; but the realisation has come not through egotism but through pain. So was it with Christ's sense of His own holiness. It woke through an attempt to stifle it. It brought to Jesus not a sense of superiority, but a sense of solitude. He felt Himself to be standing apart. The cry in Gethsemane is His cry for communion with the *world*—with those whom the Father had not yet given Him. It comes from a void in His heart. He possesses something which He wants to share; it pains Him to possess it alone. The attitude of the world threatens to perpetuate His solitude; it is aiming to destroy both Him and His possession. The Son of Man is menaced with eternal separation from the sons of men; and His prayer to the Father is a prayer for the breaking of His solitude. He is conscious of breathing a Divine air; but the consciousness comes to Him not from the sense of majesty, but from man's effort to stifle His breathing.

MY soul, hast thou considered these words, 'Could ye not watch with me one hour!' It is like the head-nurse in a hospital rebuking the sleep of the under-

nurses. In the great Hospital of Time, Jesus
was keeping watch by the couch of a sick
world. In the same˙ ward, with the same
patient to take care of, His disciples had fallen
asleep. He said to them, He says to thee,
'Couldst thou not watch with me one hour!'
What He asks from thee is no sentimental
sympathy; it is sympathy in a cause. He
does not ask, 'Dost thou feel *for* me?' He
asks, 'Dost thou feel *with* me?' Wouldst
thou have communion with Jesus; then must
thou share the *watch* of Jesus! The communion *He* desires is a community of object.
He wants thee to have a kindred taste with
Him—to love what He loves, to hate what He
hates. It is a small thing to Him that thou
shouldst cry 'Lord, Lord!' His question to
thee is, 'Canst thou drink of my cup?' His
cup is to watch by the sick-bed of the world.
Canst thou join Him, O my soul? Canst
thou pace with Him the wards of time? Canst
thou watch with Him in the infirmary of
broken hearts? Canst thou bind with Him
the wounds of the fallen? Canst thou heal

with Him the bruises of those beaten in the
world's battle?   Canst thou calm with Him
the nerves unhinged by life's fitful fever?
Canst thou even keep awake through the
night in sympathy with His vigil?   Then, in
the days to come, shall thy Father say to
thee, 'Did I not see thee in the Garden with
Him!'

CHAPTER XVIII

GETHSEMANE—*Continued*

THERE is one remaining question which must be answered ere we quit the Garden. What was the ultimate issue of this sorrow of Jesus? Was His prayer for the passing of the cup granted or rejected? It is frequently referred to as one of those petitions which have been denied. But a very early authority, a man who stands in the very front of the gallery, has taken the opposite view; and as that view is supported by the subsequent demeanour of Jesus Himself, I adopt it without hesitation. The witness of whom I speak is the writer of the Epistle to the Hebrews. He declares in the most explicit terms that the prayer of Jesus was answered, 'He was heard in the thing He feared.'

Any one who thinks that the cup from which

Jesus shrank was the fact of dying must find in these words the wildest of paradoxes. If *death in the abstract* was the thing He feared, then He was *not* heard in that thing. The cup of death was not averted from Him; He went out from the Garden to the grave. It is clear that, in the view of this writer, the thing Jesus feared was *not* death in the abstract. It was a fear of a different kind—a fear associated with the prospect of His death, but separable from it—a cup which could be removed even while the cup of death remained. Can we conceive such a dread; can we figure such a cup? That is the question I have tried to answer in last chapter. I have expressed my conviction that the thing which made Jesus recoil from the prospect of His own death was the fear lest His reconciling work should be crushed by the world's culminating sin of crucifying 'the Holy One of God.' *This* was the danger, in the dread of which He breathed the prayer, 'Father, if it be possible, let this cup pass from me!'

Now, *was* this prayer answered? *The writer*

to the Hebrews says it was. But, waiving the writer to the Hebrews, we have a yet stronger testimony—Jesus Himself. We see Him before He enters the solitude; His soul is filled with heaviness. We see Him for a time in the *midst* of the solitude; and the drops of anguish are falling from His brow. We see Him emerging from the solitude; and, lo! all is changed! His step is elastic, His eye serene, His air confident! Death is nearer to Him than ever, but He is undismayed! He repudiates the thought that the surrender to death is involuntary. He maintains that it is an act of His own will, 'Thinkest thou that I cannot now pray to my Father, and He shall presently give me more than twelve legions of angels!' He says it is His own will just because He has found it to be the will of His Father, 'The cup which my Father hath given me to drink, shall I not drink it!' Even in His moment of anguish He had expressed His willingness to take the cup of death provided only He knew that it was a part of God's plan, that it was not simply the will of the *world*. He had said, ' If this cup may not pass from me except I drink it '—if it is no human accident but something designed as a part of the picture, ' Thy will be done! ' And now He has solved that question. He has found the taking of the cup of death to be the will of His Father, and therefore it has become *His* will. He has found that this cup is no longer the cup He dreaded. It has not passed from *Him* ; but something has passed from *it*. He has been ' heard in the thing He feared.' His prayer has been answered— answered before He emerged from the solitude —answered in a way that makes Him come out stronger than He went in. Something must have occurred between the agony and the exit—something to clear the air, something to lift the heart. What was it ?

In the great gallery it is portrayed physically. We see an angel flying through the night, bearing on his wings a Divine message to Jesus. To us the interesting thing is not the angel but the message. Let us open it. We can only do so in fancy. We have no

record of the words; we are merely told that
the message brought *strength* to Jesus. But
we know what was the ground of His *weakness*.
It was His pain, His sympathy with the
Father's pain, in seeing about to be perpetrated
the culminating act of the world's sin. If this
was the source of weakness, we can imagine
what His message of strength would be.
May not we render it thus: 'My beloved Son,
this moral pain of Thine for the world's unrighteousness is to me the sweetest music. It
is the music I have long waited for, long
listened for in vain. It outweighs all the
discord; it prevails over all the jarring. I
have brought Thee to this hour that I may
hear Thy music. Thy pain for this dark
deed is itself my rainbow in the flood; Thy
beauty has condoned the deformities of men.'

I find such an assurance as this quite necessary to account, not only for the demeanour
of Jesus immediately afterwards, but for His
whole future demeanour. We shall never
again, in my opinion, see any sign in Him of
mentally sinking under His sorrow. I say,

mentally. The flesh may remain weak *after* the spirit is willing; or, to speak more correctly, the depression of the spirit may tell upon the body even after that depression is cured. In point of fact, the only trace of this struggle which the future scenes of the gallery reveal appears in the *physical* nature of Jesus. As yet the physical nature has exhibited no weakness. His bodily strength contrasts favourably with that of His disciples. When He returns to the spot where He had left Peter, James, and John, He finds them asleep. He had set them to watch for, and to report, the approach of enemies; He did not wish to be seen by these enemies in an attitude of sorrow. As a matter of fact, it is *His* eye and not theirs that detects the foe; it is *His* voice and not theirs that gives the alarm, 'He is at hand that doth betray me.'

Then follows a scene of dramatic interest. Rome and Judea gather round the Galilean. The one is represented by the swords of a cohort, the other by the staves of a Levite band. By the gleam of torches the secular

and the sacred powers come out in battle
array to fight the Man of Sorrows! They
have *expected* a fight; they have not dreamed
that Jesus would have a guard so small. Small
as it is, that guard is prepared to do battle
—not in despair, but in perfect confidence of
victory. They are but eleven in number, but
their Leader makes a twelfth; and that twelfth
is the fourth man of Daniel's furnace! They
who go with *Him* can receive no hurt! He
can cast out devils; He can tread down
scorpions! With *Him* as leader the little
band need fear no legions, no armies! Let
Him but give the word, and they will fight, and
conquer! Already a sword is drawn; already
an advance is made! Suddenly, from that
Leader a word of command does come forth;
but it is the opposite word to that for which
they have waited. It is not the signal of battle;
it is not the call to scatter their enemies; it is
the awful mandate, 'Let us surrender!'

A strange scene then presents itself. Amid
the gleaming torches, under the moonlit sky,
the cohort advances to arrest Jesus and His

band.   Jesus awaits their coming; but He
awaits them alone.   In a moment, in the
twinkling of an eye, the league of pity is dissolved!   With ignominious haste, with abject
fear, without casting a glance behind them,
the eleven flee—flee, to a man!   The higher
and the lower disciples are at last united—in
a common degradation; the jealousy of Judas
has its wish fulfilled!   They had striven who
should be nearest their Leader; the strife now
is, who shall be farthest away!   It seemed in
that moment as if the first were about to be
made last.   Nay, it appeared for an instant
as if the converse were to be also true—as if
the last were to be made first.   As the Roman
escort emerges from the Garden bearing Jesus
as their prisoner, a nameless young man follows the august Captive for a few steps of
the way.   It is but for a few steps; the officers
lay their hands upon his garment; he *leaves*
it in their hands, and flees.   Yet these few
steps were in the track of the Lord Jesus on
His road to the cross, and they have deserv-
edly made this young man, though nameless,

immortal! He did what the men of the Garden failed to do—he made an effort *not* to flee. His admiration for Jesus carried him for a few moments into fellowship with His cross, and, spite of the travesty which completes the story, these brief moments of fellowship shall be counted to him for righteousness.

The league of pity, as I have said, was for the time dissolved. It had yielded to panic. True, the germs of reconstruction were there; and reconstruction came. Panic is like a flood; it covers, but it does not necessarily destroy. These men still retained Mount Ararat below the waters, and, when the waters passed, they again rested there. Yet, for the moment Jesus was more alone than He had ever been. On this side of death He never met that league of pity as a united body again. On this side of death He never with the human eye saw more than two of its members, and on *these* His gaze rested but for a moment. Truly, if the *fault* of the band was great, it brought to them the penalty of a great privation!

Perhaps, instead of wasting time in recrimination, it will be more profitable to ask wherein lay the weakness of these men. I have said they were under the influence of panic. The question is, Why? Why did these disciples, who had received so many exceptional privileges, show to such disadvantage in the hour of danger? The common answer will be, their faith failed them. Strictly speaking, I do not think this is correct. I believe that at the time of their flight every man of that company had the same confidence in the power of Jesus which he had when he entered the Garden. When Peter drew his sword and made an actual assault on the foe he was not trusting in any power but the power of Jesus. He showed at that moment very *great* faith. Did he imagine that the natural power of the eleven was any match for the strength of a Roman cohort? Assuredly not. Why, then, did he attempt to wage so unequal a war? Because he was not *looking* to the natural power of the eleven. He was looking simply and solely to the *super*natural power of the

twelfth Man. Every other element was dis-
counted. The weakness of his own band and
the strength of the opposing band went equally
for nothing in the presence of the fact that
Jesus was there. Here is a strange psycho-
logical study! In the moment immediately
preceding their abject cowardice, Peter and
those beside him had the most absolute, the
most uncompromising faith that Jesus possessed an unlimited physical power. Why,
then, in the next instant did their faith die?

I answer, it did not die; it remained where
it was; but it was no longer available. They
believed as firmly as ever in Christ's unlimited
physical power; but He had refused to use it.
A new kind of faith was demanded of them—
faith in an unseen force which moved without
sound, assailed without weapons, conquered
without strife. They had no experience of
such a force—such a power of the spirit. To
them the glory of Jesus was the glory of
manifestation. They had lived in an atmosphere of physical wonders. They had seen
their Master in visible contact with visible

ills. They had seen Him heal the sick, cleanse
the leper, calm the demoniac, light the blind.
They had believed in His power to do these
things; they believed in it still. But that
was a power addressed to the senses, testified
to by the senses. That there existed in the
soul of Jesus a power over men which the
senses could not recognise, that there lay in the
bosom of Jesus a reserve strength of miraculous
energy which could influence the mind of man
where no outward hand appeared — this was
a thought which they had not yet conceived.
It was a thing they had not been accustomed
to. That strength should emerge from *physical
weakness* seemed to them a contradiction in
terms. They could understand how Jesus
could *dominate* the weak in body; but that
Jesus Himself should *become* weak in body
and still retain His *power*, was an idea which
transcended the utmost flight of their fancy!

And yet within a few days these men are
to *reach* that height! Within a few days they
are to scale that ascent which here, in the
Garden, is impossible to them, and are to

plant their feet upon a purely spiritual faith! It is one of the most remarkable facts of all history. No transformation is perhaps so wonderful—not even that of Saul of Tarsus! The transformation of Saul was but the transplanting of a fine intellect from one piece of ground into another. But within a few days *these* men were to experience not merely the transplanting but the actual *birth* of an intellect—the transformation of natures purely physical into minds whose bent was to be distinctly inward, and whose belief was to rest in a house not made with hands. Can we explain this marvellous change? Can we account for a transformation so remote from all analogy, so contrary to all expectancy, so inexplicable on any known principle of development? We can only explain it on the supposition that between the night of the betrayal and the dawn of the new consciousness something intervened—something in the sphere of physical fact itself which revealed to these external minds the power of the spirit in the absence of the flesh.

FORBID, O Lord, that after being with Thee in the Garden I should desert Thee in the public street! Often have I been guilty of that sin. I have gone into Thy temple to worship; I have sung hymns to Thy praise; I have breathed prayers in Thy name. But, when I have come out into the world, when I have seen the flaring torches of popular and brilliant vices, I have yielded to the spell. At such times, O Lord, send me *dis*comfort! There are seasons when Thy best gift is pain. When I have fled from Thee, send me Thy gift of pain! I have heard men say, 'There is life for a look at the crucified One.' Yes; but to Peter the life of that look came in bitter tears. So let it be with me when I forget that I am of Galilee! Send forth from Thy presence a Divine unrest! Let the evidence of Thy nearness be my own disquiet! Let the proof of Thy continued interest be the tossing of my soul! Let the dove find no rest outside the ark! When I imitate the tones of vice, let my Galilean accent betray me! For indeed I *am* of Galilee—even when

I flee! The memories of the Garden are too strong for me; they pull me back, they will not let me go. I cannot break Thy bands asunder, nor cast Thy cords from me; Thou that sittest in the heavens shalt *laugh* at my efforts to get free! Ever hold my spirit in these golden bands!

CHAPTER XIX

THE MENTAL EFFECT OF GETHSEMANE

As the stream begins to find that its course is coming into contact with the great world, I must be careful to avoid side issues. I must remember that I am not writing of the world but of the stream. On the banks of the stream there will stand immediately the representatives of nearly all ranks and conditions of men. The Jew and the Gentile will be there ; the priesthood and the empire will be there ; the soldier and the civilian will be there. Peter and John will be there to represent the apostles. The female gate-keepers of the judgment-hall will be there to represent the slave. Barabbas will be there to represent the man of revolution. The malefactor of the cross will be there to speak for the criminal classes. Humanity is indeed

powerfully represented on the banks of that
stream! Yet most of the figures must on this
occasion be ignored. My subject is the stream
itself, and I am unwilling to divert attention
from it by considering the forms of men and
women whom it passes on its way.

In the previous chapter I pointed out that
something occurred in Gethsemane to inspire
Jesus with mental, as distinguished from
physical, strength; the spirit became willing
even while the flesh remained weak. Re-
serving our consideration of the bodily element,
we will here confine ourselves to the invigorat-
ing influence on the *mind* of Jesus of that
message which He received from His Father.
We have seen that the change from depression
to confidence displayed itself in the moment
of His rejoining the disciples. But it was no
evanescent impulse. From the instant it came
to Him in the Garden it never left Him; the
spirit of fear was permanently dead; the
spirit of cloudless confidence abode with Him
till the earthly close.

Now, here is one of the most remarkable

features of the Portrait of Jesus. Let us stand
for a little in the great gallery and mark the
contrast between His aspect and His surroundings. The outward sun, the sun of His
fortunes, is very low. Never has the environment looked so dark. There is but a step
between Him and death, and that step is
inevitable. One by one the trophies which
had greeted the morning of His mission have
faded. The hosannahs are hushed; the palm-
leaves are withered; the friends of summer
days have made their flight in the winter. He
is standing before human tribunals—mocked,
reviled, buffeted. The multitude who yesterday had spread their garments for His feet,
the crowd who a few hours ago had cried,
'Blessed is He that cometh in the name of the
Lord!' are now shouting with equal lustiness,
'Away with him; let him be crucified!' He
is betrayed by one of His innermost circle;
He is deserted by all the others of that circle.
Literally at this moment He is standing alone
—unsupported by one human friend. Truly
the environment of the picture is very dark!

But now comes the strange thing. In this hour of darkness the eye of Jesus gleams with an unwonted majesty. Majesty had not been its characteristic ; in the days of His power He had been more the lamb than the lion. But in His day of weakness the lion appears. Every step of that day is a step of royalty, every word the word of a king. His assertions of power seem to grow in extent and vehemence in proportion as the shades of the prison-house close over Him. It is an experience to which I can adduce no individual parallel. I know nothing like it in the lives of *men* ; I know only one thing like it in the lives of nations—the experience of that Jewish race from which His human nature came—the experience of that race whose loudest claims to empire were uttered amid the chains of her captivities !

The briefest examination of the facts reveals this paradox in the life of Jesus. On the night of His arrest He is hurried before a meeting of the Sanhedrin on a charge of blasphemy. He is asked what He has to say to the charge ;

He utters no response ; He refuses to plead.
Why?   Is it because the forms of law have not
been complied with?   It is true they have not
been complied with ; the Sanhedrin could not
legally try a capital charge by night.[1]   But
Jesus cared too little about legal forms to be
influenced by such a consideration.   Why,
then, in answer to the reiterated questions of
Caiaphas, does He remain persistently silent?
Not because He is being illegally tried, but
because, from *His* point of view, these men
had no right, on this charge, to be His judges
at all.   I connect His silence with words He
had lately uttered, ' Henceforth I shall not
talk much with you, for the prince of this
world cometh and hath nothing in *me.*'   He
would have said that a man should be tried
by his peers—those who have something in
common with him.   What did these men
know of the region where *He* dwelt—the
house of the Father?   Nothing; they had
never been there.   And having never been
there, what right had they to judge as to His

[1] Cf. Acts ii. 23, ' Him ye have crucified by *lawless* hands.'

truth when He described the courts of heaven and the mansions of His Father's house! The silence of Jesus was a silence of majesty. He claimed to have direct communion with His Father; and He declined to have His knowledge tested by those who had only received God's message through a sighing of the wind. He demanded to be tried by His *peers*!

And in point of fact it is only when Caiaphas evokes a higher tribunal that Jesus at last breaks silence. When the High Priest says, 'I adjure thee by the living God!' he summons Jesus by another than any earthly authority. And then in answer to the bar, not of earth, but of heaven, Jesus makes that claim which constitutes the most startling event of history, 'From this time forth ye shall see the Son of Man sitting at the right hand of the power of God!'

'From this time forth.' It is as if He had said: 'I proclaim from this date the beginning of a new epoch—a humanitarian epoch. The symbols of Divine power have hitherto been animal symbols · Judea has had her lion and

Rome her eagle—the types of physical power. But from this night I proclaim the advent of a new symbol—the symbol of human sacrifice. Hitherto the sacrificial life has been the despised life ; the cross has been a mark of obloquy. From this night onward it will be a mark of glory. The test of power will henceforth be the strength of sacrifice, and men will measure nearness to God by nearness to *me.*'

What is this statement of Jesus? It is the prophecy, nay, the inauguration, of a new priesthood. I have called His Cross the fourth scene of the communion. The first was the Passover, where He communed with bygone days. The second was the Last Supper, where He held converse with His present disciples. The third was the Garden, where He stretched out His arms to the existing world of sin. The advance to the Cross was the beginning of a fourth communion, in which He was to draw to Himself the future ages. It had its fitting commencement in the vision of a true priesthood. He

was now in the presence of a false priesthood.
Caiaphas was the foil that suggested by contrast the advent of a purer ministry. *There*
lay the sting to Caiaphas. A man, a man of
the secular caste, a man without priestly orders,
a man who was only ordained after the pattern
of Melchizedek, declared that he would take
the place of the existing clerical power! He
would raise the tottering temple of Jerusalem
on a new basis—the basis of his own broken
body! The High Priest rent his clothes and
shouted, 'Blasphemy! what further need have
we for witnesses, now that we have *heard*
his blasphemy!' The subservient Council responded, 'He is worthy of death.'

The Sanhedrin gave the verdict; but they
could not give the sentence. They had no
power to inflict death; that belonged to Rome.
Accordingly, the scene changes. Jesus is led
from the Sanhedrin to the Prætorium—from
the High Priest, Caiaphas, to the Procurator,
Pontius Pilate. In passing from Caiaphas to
Pilate He has passed from the hands of the
priesthood into the hands of the empire. It is

a new atmosphere, and the old charge cannot
breathe in it.   The accusation which served
Caiaphas will have no weight with Pilate.
The Sanhedrin must transform the war-cry,
'Blasphemy against God!' into 'Treason
against Cæsar!'   Accordingly, there is no
talk here about the religious danger of the
Jewish state.   In the presence of Pilate the
Sanhedrin are only solicitous for the *Roman*
state.   They charge Jesus, not with that for
which they had condemned Him, but with
something whose gravity Pilate might be expected to appreciate—the forbidding to pay
tribute.   What *prevents* Pilate from appreciating the gravity of the charge?   It is the
seeming impotence of the defendant.   He
looks at the meek and somewhat worn countenance of the prisoner at his bar, and, in what
I take to be an accent of sarcasm, he says,
'Art *thou* the king of the Jews?'   It is this
accent of sarcasm which to my mind explains
the strange question put by Jesus in reply.
He inquires whether Pilate had asked this
of his own accord or been directed to ask it.

In other words, I understand Him to mean, 'Do you ask in order to obtain evidence, or is it a mere soliloquy of personal amusement?'

Then came the answer of Jesus to the question of Pilate, and it must have astonished him still more: 'Thou sayest it; I *am* a king. I am of royal blood; I was born to be a king; I came into the world to be a king. Yet my kingdom is not temporal; it uses no carnal weapons; it employs no physical force. Nay, it is a kingdom of sacrifice—of obedience to truth; I am come to be a *martyr* to the truth.'

It seems to me that these words of Jesus must have *caught* Pilate. There is something Roman about them. That a king should be a martyr, in other words, that a sovereign should be the servant of his country, was an idea deeply woven in the constitution of the Roman state. Cæsar himself was ideally only the head of a *republic*, and therefore in the literal sense its chief *minister*. That an empire should exist for the sake of a truth was also Roman; Rome herself had professed to live for an idea—the idea of law or justice. Pilate must have felt respect for one whose eye could thus commune with the future and recognise the permanent element in the history of nations. I think, too, when Jesus said, ' Thou wouldst have no power over me except it were given thee of God,' Pilate must have felt a Roman pride. Did not Rome wish to base her authority upon the will of heaven! Was it not her joy and her glory to proclaim the Divinity of her mission! Had not her poets sought to trace her origin to the fountain of Divine power! All this may have impressed Pilate. *Something* impressed him. He made strenuous efforts to save the prisoner. He asserted his belief in the innocence of Jesus. He washed his hands of His condemnation. He offered, in accordance with a custom of the Feast, to make Him the pardoned prisoner of that year. Four times he repeated the offer; four times was he borne down by the clamour of the crowd demanding the privilege for another man. The Roman and the Jew contended a while for the body of Jesus—the Roman for His life, the

Jew for His death—till the former was at length overborne by the cry, 'Not this man, but Barabbas!'

The multitude that shouted for Barabbas was the same multitude which at the beginning of the week had shouted for Jesus. Whence this fickleness? Had they changed their minds? No; they had at the beginning mistaken Jesus *for* Barabbas. Barabbas was a leader of sedition; they had thought Jesus a leader of sedition too. It was this that had made them strew His path with palm-leaves, and spread their garments in His way. It was this that had made them cry, 'Hosanna to the Son of David!' It was this that had evoked their hymn of praise, 'Blessed is He that cometh in the name of the Lord!' Jesus had accepted their tribute, knowing that His power was higher than they dreamed of; but, so far as *their* consciousness extended, it was only a tribute to Barabbas. They were seeking a leader of sedition in Jesus or another; when they failed to find one in Jesus, they *turned* to another. They saw in Barabbas what they had thought to find in Jesus—a revolutionary man, a lawless man, a man who might lead his countrymen to a kingdom of flesh and blood. Jesus was above their expectations; He wanted things too high for them. Barabbas was on a level with their imaginings; he wanted only purple and fine linen and sumptuous faring every day; therefore the roar for Barabbas drowned the murmur for Jesus!

And Pilate yielded to their clamour; he gave up the Christ to die. Looking back through the years, what shall be our estimate of the comparative guilt of Pilate and Caiaphas? to which shall we assign the greater blame? Christendom both ancient and modern has been prone to give the foremost place in wickedness to Caiaphas—to look upon Pilate with a more lenient eye. In that feeling I cannot concur. So far as the condemning of Jesus is concerned, I think Pilate much the worse of the two. Caiaphas really believed that Jesus would hurt him—and, from a selfish point of view, he was right in his belief; Pilate had *nothing* to fear from Jesus, and he did fear nothing. The claim of Jesus before the tribunal of Caiaphas menaced the Jewish state; the claim of Jesus before the tribunal of Pilate did not menace the *Roman* state. To Caiaphas the attitude of Jesus was a serious matter vitally affecting the national faith. To Pilate the attitude of Jesus was the subject for a jest. Each of these men was condemning Jesus on his own separate charge—Caiaphas for blasphemy, Pilate for treason. Both men were to some extent false; but they were not equally false. Caiaphas was false to this extent, that he only *pretended* to believe in the *treason*; but he had this much truth, that he really believed in the *blasphemy*. Pilate, on the other hand, believed in neither charge; he was convinced that both were baseless. Yet Pilate condemned Jesus. He yielded to a popular clamour—yielded for the sake of his own interest. He was there to administer public law; he gave a verdict from motives of private advantage. He was there to represent Roman justice; what he did represent was the lowest form of humanity in any land—the class who sell their conscience in truckling for popular favour.   The more Pilate was influenced by the presence of Jesus, the darker is the aspect in which his deed appears, for there is no sin equal to a sin against light.   There is no moral miracle of Christ which surpasses in range of power the fact that in the hour of His humiliation He could influence a man so sordid as Pilate!

L ORD, help me to see Thy power in the day when men arraign Thee!   We still place Thee at the bar of our judgment-seat; we still accuse Thee before our Pilate and our Caiaphas.   We point to what we call the weak spots in Thy government.   Teach me Thy *strength* in these spots!   Let me learn the majesty of Thy power in the paths where men despise Thee!   Let me hear Thy songs in the *night*; let me see Thy bow in the *cloud*!   When Thy cause seems trampled down and when I seem crushed along with Thee, let Thy words reach my ear, 'I *am* a king'!   They can only reach my ear by reaching my heart. I shall know *Thy* strength by *my* strength. I shall know Thy strength by my unaccountable peace, by my inexplicable calm. I shall know it 'by the gleam and glitter of the golden chain I wear'—the gleam and glitter that have come from the furnace of fire. I shall know it by the Pisgah heights that greet the declining sun, by the streams that surprise me in the desert, by the gates which open to me in the enclosing wall. I shall know it by the proof of the promise, 'As thy days, so shall thy strength be!'

CHAPTER XX

THE PHYSICAL EFFECT OF GETHSEMANE

THE grief of the Garden affected Jesus both in soul and body. His soul was 'exceeding sorrowful,' and His bodily sweat was like 'great drops of blood falling to the ground.' There is indicated in the statement at once a mental and a physical influence. The inner and the outer life were equally depressed by the overwhelming weight of His sufferings. Then, as we have seen, there intervened something. A great strength descended on His spirit. He received a message from His Father which sent His heart up like the lark. From that moment He was mentally lifted up for ever. But His body did not rise simultaneously with His spirit. When the body and the spirit are depressed together through the presence of a grief, it does not follow that the removal of the grief will *raise* them together. We have experience of the contrary. When we are relieved from the grinding at any mill, one part of us is taken and the other left. The part taken—taken up into joy, is the spirit; the body remains a while on the ground. How often our health breaks down after the time of crisis is happily past! This could not be if the body had shared simultaneously in the rise of the spirit. It is a law of human nature that the physical man shall continue to bear the suffering of the Garden after the inward man has been set free.

In the case of Jesus there was an additional reason why the elevation of His spirit did not at once affect the outward frame. The joy which came to Him in the Garden was a purely spiritual joy. It was not justified by any change in the environment. It was a peace that passed understanding. Nothing had happened to account for it; nothing followed to vindicate it. The Garden remained where it was; its outward cause of grief remained where it was; the cup of physical death, so far as it could be measured by the eye, was as full as ever. It was only from the soul that a weight had really been lifted. The joy of the Garden could exert upon the body only a negative influence. In the absence of a physical change all that it could do was to retard the advance of weakness, to delay somewhat the collapse of the outward form.

From the moment of leaving the Garden everything conspired to hasten this collapse. Jesus was subjected to a series of physical strains involving successive marchings, prolonged wakefulness, sustained attention of eye and ear. After the cold night-vigil of Gethsemane He is led through the streets at midnight to the hall of judgment. With unseemly, with illegal haste, the events that should have occupied days are crowded into hours. With hardly an interval between He is brought before a succession of tribunals. I omitted to detail these in the previous chapter because I wanted to direct attention rather to the settled attitude of Christ's mind than to the shifting nature of His fortunes. But when we speak of the physical in Jesus these fatiguing experiences, coming as they do after the depression of the Garden, have a deep significance in explaining the collapse that was to come. The process must have been one of extreme outward exhaustion. First He is examined before Annas; then He stands before the bar of Caiaphas; then He is placed at the judgment-seat of Pilate; then He is sent to Herod; lastly, for final sentence, He is sent back to Pilate again. Then follows the condemnation to be crucified. Instantly He becomes the target for disrespect—legal and popular; for death by the cross was itself a badge of disgrace. Pilate scourges Him; the multitude insult and mock and buffet Him. Then He is brought forth to the streets again, and the procession begins to move toward the final scene. They ascend the Dolorous Way leading their august Captive to His destined doom; and that Captive Himself, in accordance with the custom on such occasions, carries His own cross.

Suddenly something happens—something which we can only see through a veil. The narrative only reveals it dimly; but it has been vividly painted by the pencil of Albrecht Dürer. Jesus faints under His burden. He can go no farther; His physical strength is at last exhausted and He sinks beneath the weight of His cross. It is transferred from Him to a commonplace man who has come out from the country districts and has joined the procession through curiosity. It is to my mind at once the most human and the most Divinely helpful incident in the whole life of Jesus. It constitutes a distinct feature in the great gallery, and it bears to the heart a message which has not been given by any other phase of the Portrait. Let us ponder for a little the depth of its revelation.

There is something peculiarly sad in a physical collapse. We see, for example, a medical student who has brilliantly passed all his examinations but one—the concluding

one for which he has not yet stood. He is
about to enter upon this final trial. He has
full confidence of success, and there opens
before him the prospect of a golden life in
the service of man. Suddenly his health
breaks down; physical faintness overtakes
him; he sinks by the wayside. At the very
moment of planting his foot upon the
threshold his foot slips and he is laid aside
from work. Just within sight of the promised
land, he is forbidden to enter in, and the
commonplace Joshua gets the niche *he* was
designed to fill.

Now, where lies the pain of this position?
In this, that the student continues to bear *in
his mind* the burden he has dropped from his
hand. He is still doing in the *spirit* the work
he is prevented from achieving in the *flesh*.
Lying on his bed of weakness, he can no
longer entertain the prospect of carrying *on
his shoulders* the cross of humanity; but the
sense of this inability is made more bitter by
the fact that he has never ceased to carry it
in his heart, and that, if he only had the

physical power, the yoke to him would be easy and the burden light.

Now, excluding the bitterness, this is the position of the human soul of Jesus at the stage where we have arrived. Do not be afraid of the earthly analogy; the doctrine of Incarnation justifies all analogies. Jesus has been sweeping all difficulties before Him. He has stood the ordeal of what I may reverently call successive examinations. He has passed the examination by Annas, by Caiaphas, by Herod, by Pilate. He has but one more to undergo—the examination by the crowd who stand to witness His progress up the Dolorous Way! As He passes before them bearing His physical burden, His outward strength succumbs. The cross drops from His weary frame. He is unable to complete the outward task; a commonplace man has to finish it for Him. And all the rest of that journey up that Dolorous Way Jesus has to bear His burden *only in the spirit.* The cross of humanity is still carried in His *heart*; but it is there alone. He has been constrained to give up external work. His labours for humanity live, for the time, only in His sympathy. He performs them merely in His heart, in His wish, in His will. The spirit alone is ready, the flesh is weak.

Have you weighed the comfort which this incident must bring to every follower of Christ? Jesus is recognised as the typical bearer of the cross of humanity, as having never *paused* in that work of cross-bearing. And yet, mechanically speaking, He did pause; He became for a time an invalid; He had to pass the outward burden into the hands of another. The outward work was still imputed to Him; but why? Because He was still doing it in the spirit. Up that Dolorous Way He carried the cross only in His mind; but that mental carrying was counted to Him for an outward deed. *There* is the comfort to a follower of Jesus! When a man is laid aside from the world, prostrated on a bed of sickness, disabled from doing any work with the hand, he can appeal to his Master's experience in vindication of his own. He can plead that he is still doing the work in his heart, and that every act performed in his heart will be counted to him as equivalent to an act done outside.   He may claim, in fellowship with Jesus, that even in his hour of inaction he has been bearing his cross up the Dolorous Way.

I have said that without this incident we should not elsewhere in the Portrait meet with precisely the same suggestion.   I read lately in a book written by one of the most distinguished of living clergymen, an extraordinary statement. He said that Christ was subject to every form of human vicissitude except, perhaps, sickness. It was the exception that startled me; it seemed to impoverish, rather than enrich, the Portrait.   I set myself to inquire in the great gallery whether there was not some trace of this unobserved feature.   And I was truly glad when I found it here—on the road up to Golgotha.   The weariness at the well would not make a complete humanity if it were not supplemented by a weariness on the sick-bed. We cannot afford to part with this incident in the life of Jesus.

I have said that when Jesus dropped His outward cross it fell into the hands of a commonplace man. He is called Simon of Cyrene. Cyrene was situated in North Africa, and it contained a Jewish colony. I do not think, however, that Simon was a Jewish colonist. I think he must have belonged to the slave population. I cannot imagine that a free man would have been made the victim of such an indignity as to be forced to bear the cross of one on his way to crucifixion. The narrative distinctly points out that it was no voluntary act on his part: 'him they *compelled* to bear His cross.' There was not present at that moment a single man who would have accepted the burden with his will —probably not one that would have accepted it for hire. Jesus in His hour of sickness could find neither a hand to nurse for affection nor a hand to nurse for reward; the care He received was all the result of compulsion.

We will say, then, that Simon was an African slave. If he had the blood of North Africa in his veins, his person in the eyes of the Jew was *associated* with slavery. He came from a hated race—the race of Ham. He came from the race that, according to Jewish tradition, had received the solemn curse of the patriarch Noah, that had been doomed to the place of a servant of servants.[1] He belonged to a fraternal branch of that people which Israel had been bidden to exterminate, to expel, to root out of the land—that people from whose captives taken in war she had constituted her first ownership of a community of slaves. Doubtless such a thought was in the mind of the Jew when he compelled Simon of Cyrene to bear the cross of Jesus.

What had brought Simon there? Curiosity—tinged, no doubt, with a little complacency. Coming out from the country he had met and followed the procession—that procession which accompanied to the place of death one reported to be a lineal descendant of the royal house

[1] The condemnation to be 'a servant of servants' (Genesis ix. 25) is really intended for all Ham's posterity; it is specially associated with the name of Canaan merely because Canaan represents the *Hebrew* branch; the meaning is 'keep Ham's posterity away from *our* shores!'

of David. I can imagine, I say, that some complacency mingled with his curiosity. I can conceive him thus communing with himself: 'So this is what it has come to at last! Pride has indeed got a fall! The line of David crushed our line; where is it now! Here is the last of the series—a man broken, shattered, reviled, led to a malefactor's doom! The rose of Jesse has withered; the glory of Solomon has faded; the light of the royal line is going out in gloom! Truly the wrongs of the Canaanite have been at length avenged!'

Such, in more direct language, must have been the sentiment of the African slave as he stood, spectator of the scene. Suddenly the spectator is made an actor! A ring gathers round him. Jesus has dropped His cross through exhaustion; here is a strong, able-bodied man who can supply the vacant place! Within a few seconds Simon finds himself where Jesus stood. Reluctant, struggling, protesting, he is dragged into the arena; and the burden which has fallen from the Son of Man is laid upon *him*!

What does this mean? I do not ask what does it mean for *Simon*, but what does it mean for the *world*? I have said that the final scene in the life of Jesus embraces the many phases of His communion with future ages. We have seen in His meeting with Caiaphas and Pilate His communion with the future life of nations. What is involved in His meeting with Simon of Cyrene? It is the inauguration of something very distinct and novel. Simon is '*compelled* to bear His cross.' It is the initiation of a great fact— that henceforth the bearing of that cross will be inevitable to all. The fate of Simon is not merely historical; it is typical. It tells you and me that no man can *escape* the cross of Jesus. We may or may not commune with Jesus Himself, but we have no alternative as to communing with His *cross*. The choice is not between taking the cross of Christ or leaving it; we *must* take it. The choice is, shall we be compelled to bear it or *im*pelled to bear it; shall it be thrust upon us by law or shall it be appropriated by love? Christ has brought man so near to man that my brother cannot suffer without his suffering affecting *me*. I cannot escape the 'cross of humanity, for there has been woven a network round all men which makes it imperative they should rejoice or suffer together. One question alone awaits me—shall I let my brother's cross come to *me*, or shall I go to meet my brother's cross? Shall I be *com*pelled or shall I be *im*pelled to bear it? Shall I take it through sympathy or shall I take it like Simon of Cyrene? That is the choice, that is the alternative; other course lies before no man. Communion with the cross there *must* be, but there are two roads which lead to it; which shall be mine?

I HAVE chosen, O Lord; I shall take *love's* way. I shall not be like Simon of Cyrene —an *unwilling* burden-bearer; my service shall be free. *Still* Thou art passing up the Dolorous Way carrying the burden of Thy cross! *Still* Thou comest, footsore and weary, bearing Thy great weight — the weight of humanity! Thou hast borne it from the gates of the Garden all down the stream of Time; Thou hast carried it from the first hour of Calvary to the last hour of to-day! Shall I let Thee bear it any longer *alone*! I have seen the multitude forsake Thee. I have seen Thy disciples flee—the men of the mountain and the men of the plain together. I have seen Simon of Cyrene compelled to do with his hand a service which his heart revolted from. I cannot bear this neglect of Thee, O Lord! Give me a fragment of Thy cross! Let me *help* Thee with Thy burden up the Dolorous Way! Let me lend one touch to the lifting of the mighty load! Let me lessen by one added hand the weight of Thy labour! Let me lighten, even by one helping arm, the heaviness of the pressure on Thy heart! I would never have it said of me that I was *compelled* to bear Thy cross!

CHAPTER XXI

THE HOUR OF PRIESTHOOD

WE have in the course of these volumes seen
Jesus in two aspects—that of the prophet and
that of the king. Galilee has revealed Him
as the prophet; Jerusalem, spite of His approaching death-shadows, has revealed Him
as the king. We are now to see Him in His
third aspect—that of the priest. The distinctive hour of His priesthood has now struck.
I would place its striking precisely at that
moment when He dropped His outward cross.
That was the beginning of His absolute
passiveness. Hitherto His service of man has
been *active*; He has been the helper and the
healer. But now the surrender of His life is
to take a new form. Instead of ministering
with the hand, He is to yield Himself into
the hands of others. The last trace of active

power was the carrying of His cross up the steep of Golgotha. But now the cross has fallen to the ground; His strength is feeble; His steps are tottering; there is nothing left for Him but to die. He has been the prophet; He has been the king; He is now to be the priest surrendering the passive victim; and the passive victim is to be His own soul.

But let us remember that when the cross dropped from the shoulder it did not drop from the heart. We must never forget that the effect of Gethsemane's message upon the soul of Jesus was a permanent effect. It never deserted Him. It struck a light which remained in His sky even at His darkest hour. We shall go wrong, in my opinion, if we imagine that the Cross of Calvary was at any time to Jesus a starless night. There was dense darkness over the *earth*; but the vision of Jesus went beyond the earth. The Gethsemane message—the message which told of an accepted world, of a pardoned humanity, of a fear dispelled—never ceased ringing in His ear. It rose above the taunts, above the revilings, above the earthquake, above the rending of rocks. It made His last voice a note of triumph, but it gave strength also to His previous voices. Strength, did I say! I should have said, regalness. Nowhere is Jesus more regal than in His parting hour. Nowhere, as St. John says, does He seem more uplifted than in His passion. Nowhere is He more glorified than in His cross. And the reason is that He has been glorified *previous* to the cross—glorified by a message from His Father which has made His heart strong and given to His inner eye a mountain view.

There is a remarkable passage in a letter written by one of Christ's disciples, nay, by one who was with Him in the Garden; and it expresses the view at which we have here arrived. This disciple says that Jesus was 'put to death in the flesh but quickened in the spirit.' I understand this to mean, not merely that the spirit of Jesus was quickened *after death*, but that it was exempt from the weakness incidental to the outward frame in the process of crucifixion; the spirit remained willing even while the flesh was weak. From the very outset of this scene the attitude of Jesus is one of mental strength. He refuses to partake of a narcotic which is offered Him to dull the coming pain. Why? Did He deem that there was any advantage in physical pain? No; the whole aim of His outward ministry had been to relieve it. But He will not purchase immunity from physical pain by immunity from thought. The offered drink would have blunted consciousness. It is *from* consciousness, and not from its absence, that Jesus expects a dulling of physical pain. Two things may relieve outward suffering—an anæsthetic, or a joy. Jesus rejected the anæsthetic because He already possessed the joy. He had received in the Garden a message from His Father which was to Him more powerful than any narcotic—which lifted the burden of His pain, not by a suspension of vital energy, but by an enlargement of mental comfort.

Do you doubt that this message of the

Garden was the golden thread which encircled His cross, in other words, that before coming to Calvary He had been already 'crowned with glory and honour for the suffering of death'?   Here is the proof: in the very moment when He lay down upon that cross, in the initial moment of physical pain and outward laceration, Jesus breathed a prayer that the Father would ratify His Gethsemane message; He said, 'Father, forgive them; they know not what they do.'   In that physically dread moment, the first thing in the consciousness of Jesus was not the impression of the nails but the impression of the Garden promise. His prayer was virtually this: 'Father, fulfil to me Thy promised joy!   Ratify to me the message of the Garden!   Thou hast seen me trembling in the Garden lest this culminating deed of sin should chill Thy heart for ever. And Thou hast answered that trembling, O my Father!   Thou hast sent me a message of strength; Thou hast told me that my flower of sacrifice will outweigh the world's thorn.   Fulfil this joy, my Father!   Accept the thorn, yea, the crown of thorns, for the sake of the roses I bring! Forgive those who have raised this cross!'

You will observe here a repetition of that same regal bearing which we beheld in the Garden agony. The bodily attitude of Jesus on the cross is a prostrate attitude. But at this very moment His *soul* is standing upright. He is never more majestic than in His prayer, 'Father, forgive them; they know not what they do—they have not realised that they are attempting to destroy absolute purity.' It is the most unique exhibition of conscious moral dignity which the world has ever seen; and it is the more unique on this account, that it is entirely apart from egotism; it is used entirely in the service of others. The priesthood of Jesus on the cross never for an instant lost sight of His kinghood on the throne.

As I stand in the great gallery I am deeply impressed with the artistic effort to portray the crown of Jesus in the midst of His cross. Has it ever occurred to you to wonder why that sensuous age makes so little of the physical sufferings of Jesus? Modern preachers have painted in ghastly colours the outward agonies of Calvary. But the first narrators of the scene are dominated by the determination to tell only how the kinghood conquered the pain. I shall illustrate the point presently; meantime I am simply asking its artistic cause. And that cause is not far to seek. There can be no expiation in mere physical pain. Legal penalty there may be, but not expiation. Expiation demands an act of will. However complete be the surrender, it must be a conscious surrender, a voluntary surrender. The expiating work of Jesus, whether in life or in death, is not the fact that He lay passive in the hand of the Father; it is His *determination* to lie passive. In life and in death alike the source of expiation is not the impotence, but the regal strength, of Jesus—the fact that He could say, 'No man taketh my life from me; I lay it down of myself; I have power to lay it down and I have power to take it again.'

That is the reason why in the great gallery

so little prominence is given to the physical pain of Jesus. It is designed that even on the cross He should verify His words to Pilate, ' I *am* a king.' Accordingly, the attitude of Jesus on the cross is not that of an abject victim. We listen in vain for any expression of physical suffering.[1] No groan escapes Him; no cry of anguish reaches our ear; as a sheep dumb before its shearers He opens not His mouth. We feel as if His personal life were already buried, as if the wants of His body were forgotten in the wants of love. Where His silence is broken it is never to utter a complaint; it is always to express an *im*personal interest. It would seem as if the print of the nails had impressed upon His human organism not His own pains but the pains of others. Explain it as you will, these hours of Calvary are to Him not a season of individual weeping but a season of universal communion. Solitary as He personally was, His cross was the focus of humanity. Round it there gathered the representatives of every class—the slave, the

---

[1] Unless St. John xix. 28 be counted as such.

peasant, the priest, the scribe, the soldier, the malefactor, the disciple, the woman. And to the eye of the narrator, these are the subjects of the coming empire—the future servants in whose midst and in whose interest the lonely and prostrate Sufferer legislates as a king.

What other thought than this is in the mind of the evangelist when he records that above the cross of Jesus there was placarded an inscription written in Greek and Latin and Aramaic: 'This is Jesus the King of the Jews'! I am aware that Pilate wrote it in mockery, or at least, in cynicism. But what he said in jest the evangelist received in earnest and posterity has realised as fact. Aramaic, Greek, Latin— the language of the people, the language of the cultured, the language of the military—that Passion Week Jesus had heard them all. He had heard the hosannas of the Jewish rabble; He had received the mission of the cultured Greeks; He had listened to the voice of the Roman soldiers. And the evangelist felt, nay, Jesus felt, that these three representative voices would be raised for the Christ of the future.

In the coming age His gospel would influence all the three—the men who toil, the men who study, the men who fight ; it would support the first, it would illuminate the second, it would soften the third. This has been the actual course of Christianity. It has secured the rights of the masses ; it has trimmed the lamp of the student ; it has mitigated the horrors of war. Is there in the mind of the narrator some prophetic foresight of this last point when he tells us that Christ's garment was parted among the soldiers? It was the custom at such times ; but to the eye of His followers Christ's contact invested every old custom with a new significance. Did not the new significance of this distribution lie in the belief that the Roman soldier was unconsciously being clothed upon by a new spirit, and being invested with a garment whose power of creating inward warmth would be learned by him in after years?

Presently there occurred an incident which establishes beyond all controversy the regal character of the scene depicted in the gallery.

In the very act of crucifixion, in the very
moment of physical prostration, Jesus received
a tribute of homage equal to anything which
had marked the days of His power. It came
from the lips of a malefactor who was being
crucified along with Him. In the last hour of
a bad life this dying criminal raised his eyes in
prayer to his Fellow-Sufferer and cried, 'Lord,
remember me when Thou comest in Thy kingdom!' He received more than he asked. He
asked to obtain salvation in the far future;
Jesus offered it then and there, 'Verily I say
unto thee, "to-day shalt thou be with me in
Paradise"'1

The incident is commonly used by preachers
to exemplify the possibility of an extraordinary
exercise of Divine mercy. That this man
should gain in a moment what a Peter secured
only after long and violent struggle seems a
thing that can be accounted for by nothing
else than a miraculous stretch of pardon. And
yet, to think so is a great mistake. The
miraculous thing is not the pardon, but the
ripeness, of the malefactor. There are flowers

in the American prairies that spring up in a
single night. When they do spring up, they
are entitled to all the *benefits* of a flower; it is
no *miracle* that they drink the sunshine. The
whole wonder lies in their quick springing, in
the acceleration of their development. So is it
with this malefactor. The marvel is the ripeness of his faith. You say he received a
quicker reward than Peter. He deserved it.
He displayed exactly that kind of faith which
Peter in the Garden had failed to reach—faith
in Christ's power on the *cross*. His spiritual
life was *born* on Calvary; he was the first leaf
of that winter tree. He came to Jesus in His
human poverty. He came to Him when, to
the eye of sense, He was a dying man. He
came to Him when He had been divested of
every robe which meant royalty, denuded of
every badge which declared Him to be a
king. And yet, in that hour he perceived His
royalty. He detected the gold beneath the
dust; he recognised the kingdom through the
cloud. In the absence of all visible glory, in
the presence of all that suggested humiliation,

this man discerned a regal majesty, a power to which in death a human soul might pray. And Jesus discerned in *him* the presage of His coming kingdom—the first-fruits of a great communion in which the voices of a responsive multitude should break the solitude of the Son of Man.

I have always felt that this malefactor on the cross is the extreme antithesis to the portrait of Judas. They both teach the same moral—that a man can only be converted from within ; but Judas teaches it by his failure, the malefactor by his success. Judas had from the beginning every outward advantage. He saw the Master in His physical glory ; he lived in a sanctified environment. But there was no response from the *inner* man, and therefore all the environment went for nothing. The malefactor, on the other hand, had no outward advantages. His had been an environment of evil. He had lived in a debased atmosphere ; he had only seen Jesus at the last hour. Yet there was in him something which was independent of environment and which bad surroundings could not kill. There was an *inner* life which unconsciously waited and thirsted; and, when the well of water appeared, the thirsting soul recognised its need and ran forth spontaneously to meet the coming joy.

I THANK Thee, O Lord, that it was in Thine hour of *sacrifice* the world received Thy garment. I thank Thee that it was at Thy *cross* Thy robes were parted among men. It is Thy moment of humiliation that has reclothed humanity. There was a garment of Thine on the Mount of Transfiguration; but that has not been parted among us. I am glad *that* was not the garment chosen. It suited Thee, but it would not suit us. It was too white, too glistening, for our toilsome day. We want something that will stand the tear and wear of life, something fitted for work that soils the outer hand. And we have found it in this second garment of Thine—the garment given at Thy cross. Ever let me touch the hem of that garment, O Lord! With that robe upon me I can do all work and receive no stain. With that robe upon me I can touch impurity and still be pure. With that robe upon me I can touch things soiled with moth and rust; and the moth will not corrupt and the rust will not corrode. The *saints in heaven* may walk in white before Thee; but the garment for *me* is the garment of Thy cross!

CHAPTER XXII

THE HOUR OF PRIESTHOOD—*Continued*

THE point I am considering is one of artistic contrast. In the delineation of the great gallery the last hours of the Son of Man are described in a twofold aspect; the flesh is weak, but the spirit is willing. I am trying to illustrate this twofold attitude, am seeking to show how the persistent aim of those who depict Christ's death is to poise His mental strength over against His physical weakness. At the very moment when the body is prostrated, racked with pain and exhausted by fatigue, the soul of Jesus is represented in an upright posture, manifesting an active interest in things around, and exercising a regal and legislative influence in the midst of the closing scene. We have been considering one of these legislative acts—the admission of the malefactor into the kingdom of God. We are now to witness another of a different kind. The case of the malefactor was an act of jurisdiction in the sphere of the criminal; we are now to see an exercise of authority in the sphere of the household. The altar and the hearth are once more to be united, and this time they are to be joined by a reunion with His own domestic circle—the circle of His Nazareth home.

It is strange and beautiful to see the two extreme points of life thus joined. Calvary and Nazareth were very far apart, and much had intervened to separate the aspirations of the one from the hopes of the other. Yet here they met side by side. Shortly after the malefactor's prayer there stood before the cross a group of five. Four of them were women, and two of these women belonged to the family of Jesus—His mother and her sister. The fifth of the group was a man, but a man who was yet to develop a truly feminine soul; it was the disciple whom Jesus specially loved —John, son of Zebedee. As they stood below the cross, the eye of Jesus rested successively on two of them—the mother and the beloved disciple; and He committed to that disciple the greatest trust that has ever been reposed in any human being—the charge of His earthly parent, 'Woman, behold thy son; son, behold thy mother!'

There is something grand in this home touch amid the storm. There are mountains whose summits are white with the snows of winter and yet at whose base there reposes a wealth of summer flowers. Some such picture is here. The head of Jesus is crowned with thorns; but His heart reposes in the memories of home. The songs of Galilee ring in His ear *above* the tumult of Jerusalem; and He turns aside from His pain to bless the old cottage of Nazareth. The physical suffering is superseded by an act of impersonal communion. Jesus on the cross communes with the home life of coming ages. He sanctifies for all time to come the ties of the family, and puts an eternal imprimatur upon the affections of the heart.

It is curious that in the closing of St. John's

Gospel there should thus ring out the refrain of its opening pages. It begins with a domestic scene—the marriage feast of Cana, where the mother is seen standing beside her son. It closes with a scene in which the mother and son again stand side by side, and in a different shape the miracle is again performed of glorifying the commonplace—of turning the water into wine.

I am inclined to recognise another refrain of this Gospel's opening in the words which Jesus next breathes on the cross, ' I thirst !' They express the only personal want to which He there gives utterance. I have no doubt they express a *real* personal want. I have no doubt that here, as at the well of Samaria, He asked water because He wanted it. But I think that here He had the well of Samaria behind Him as a background of memory. There, in His hour of need, man had ministered to Him ; and the ministration had been sweet. *Now* there had come to Him an hour of need deeper still ; would He not give man again a chance to minister ! Real as the craving was,

I think this was the motive for expressing it. I believe that but for this motive He would never have told His want. He could have kept it within His heart; He had deeper wants than *this* within His heart, unseen, unheard, hid from the common gaze. If this is spoken out, it is not for His own sake but for the sake of Man. He wants His *brother* to offer Him the cup of cold water. He wants to receive in that cup a counterpart of the communion in the wilderness of Bethsaida. That was a gift from the hand of Jesus to the multitude; was there to be no gift from the hand of the multitude to Jesus! Was not the time come when the Son of Man should be, not the giver, but the receiver! I believe it was this thought which dictated to Jesus the one expression of physical want on the cross. The outward thirst was real; but He had an inner thirst which was deeper — the desire for human sympathy. The satisfaction of the outer thirst by the hand of Man would allay the inner craving. It would prove thè existence of compassion — a word which literally means participation in the suffering of another. Therefore it was that Jesus asked the outward draught.

And when He received it from a purely secular hand, I doubt not He received it as an act of communion. The man who gave it was to Him a representative man. He stood for the secular ages to come. He stood for those whose charity would be better than their creed, whose pity would be larger than their faith. He represented those who in future ages would help humanity without knowing that they were helping *Him*. That is why Jesus did not refuse the draught. It meant to Him more than it said. It implied, not a cup, but an ocean—not the outpouring of a little wine, but the pouring forth of a world's heart!

There is only one incident of these hours on the cross which might be thought to militate against my view that the soul of Jesus remained erect amid the stooping of the body. I allude to the words which He uttered in

soliloquy, 'My God, my God, why hast Thou
forsaken me!' They have been thought to
indicate that, for an instant at least, the spirit
of Jesus was overclouded by His sufferings,
and that the waves of a momentary despair
swept across His soul. From my point of
view such a conclusion is, of course, impossible.
I regard Christ's mental anguish as having
been conquered in *Gethsemane.* Even in Gethsemane He did not fear that the Father would
forsake *Him,* but that the Father would forsake the world. Waiving, however, any opinion
of mine in this matter, look at the record
itself! Do you think it likely that, almost
immediately after an expression of the most
cloudless confidence, almost immediately after
the triumphant declaration to the malefactor,
'To-day shalt thou be with me in Paradise,'
Jesus should have been overmastered by despair,
should have sunk into the deepest despond-
ency, should have felt Himself abandoned by
that Father in whose service He had lived
and for whose glory alone He had laboured?
Paradise was *open* to His eyes a little while

before.   Could Jesus doubt His own vision?
Could He feel uncertain about that of which
a few moments ago He was sure?   The very
statement refutes itself, nullifies itself!   We
must look *elsewhere* for an explanation of the
words, 'My God, my God, why hast Thou
forsaken me!'

Nor, do I think, need we look far for a *very*
different explanation of them.   We have to
bear in mind first of all that the words are
not an *original* utterance of Jesus; they are
a quotation from the opening of the twenty-
second Psalm.   The question therefore narrows
itself to this, Why did Jesus on this occasion
quote this Psalm?   Now observe, He was not
the only one who was quoting it.   It was
being referred to all round either by word or
deed.   The soldiers were dividing His raiment
amongst them ; what Jew could fail to read
in that action those words of that twenty-
second Psalm, 'They parted my garment
amongst them, and on my vesture they cast
lots'!   The priests were mocking Him as
they passed by; and their mockery was all

expressed in the words of that twenty-second Psalm, 'He trusted in God that He would deliver him; let Him deliver him if He delighted in him!' In other words, they said: 'Here is a man evidently forsaken by God! If he were not forsaken by God, would he have this *cross*? If God were on his side, would He allow him to be buffeted, scourged, crucified? No; he would be clothed in purple and fine linen, and would fare sumptuously every day. He would be rich; he would be strong; he would be joyful; he would be crowned with laurels. Let this man come *down* from the cross, and we shall believe in him! Let him show us his prosperity, and we shall confess that God is with him! Meantime, we know by his fallen fortunes that he is forsaken of heaven.'

Now, when everybody was quoting the Psalm, Jesus quoted it too. It was no mere imitation that made Him follow the stream. He remembered in this Psalm something which those others repeating it had forgotten. *They* were quoting it as His cry of *despair*. *He*

remembered that it was really a psalm of
hope. He uttered the first line aloud, but He
said the rest in His heart. To my mind, it
was the concluding part of the Psalm that
dominated the soul of Jesus. Read that concluding part. Read the portion extending
from the twenty-second verse to the end. Is
that the utterance of a man who thinks himself forsaken? On the contrary, it is the
greatest blast of triumph ever blown! The
message of these verses is an assertion that
the appearance of forsakenness was a delusion.
It reversed the notes with which the song
had opened; it turned the funeral march into
a bridal strain. And it was this *closing strain*
of which Jesus was thinking when He uttered
the *opening words.* He heard the end from
the beginning. The final pæan of glory rang
in His ear though He began with the minor
and mournful prelude; and while His lips
were saying, 'Why hast Thou forsaken me!'
His heart was anticipating the words, 'In
the midst of the congregation will I praise
Thee!'

The truth is, Christ's expiation was His *acquiescence* — His power to see something *beyond the pain.* Why do we not take the dying malefactor as an expiation for the sins of the world? His physical sufferings were of the same kind as those of Jesus. His cross was side by side—erected on the same spot, raised at the same moment; why do we magnify the crucified Jesus and merely pity the crucified penitent? You say, 'Jesus was Divine.' Yes; but that is a magnifying of His crown—not of His cross. The cross belongs to the *human* side. We want to know what makes the cross of the Man Christ Jesus what the cross of the penitent is *not*—an expiation for the sins of the world. 'It was because Jesus had more pain,' you say. Strange as it may seem, I think the reason is exactly the reverse. If I should not be misunderstood, I would say that Jesus had *less* physical pain, and that in this lies His power of expiation. The gift He renders to the Father is sweet in proportion as it is voluntary; it is not the agony, but the acquiescence, that

expiates the sin of the world. Even the
Jewish prophet had predicted this of the Holy
Child of God, whoever he might be, and whenever he might come, 'When Thou shalt make
His soul an offering for sin, the pleasure of
the Lord shall prosper in His hands.' If 'it
pleased the Lord to bruise Him,' what pleased
Him was not the bruises but the unconquer-
able joy. It was the persistence of love through
loss, of peace through pain, of trust through
trial, of courage through contumely, of devotion
through death. The tribute dearest to the
Father from the Cross of Calvary was not the
prostration of a body but the surrender of a
will.

And this helps us to understand why the
last scene of all is a blaze of mental triumph.
It is a blaze made all the more remarkable
by the fact that the physical surroundings
are depicted at the lowest. The great gallery
is all in gloom. Dense darkness has come
on ; the frame of the Portrait is utterly hid.
Even artificial lights cannot be procured, for
there is a trembling of the earth before which

they could not stand. Yet it is at this moment, of all moments, that the eye of Jesus gleams out with resplendent brightness. It is from the dark room, from the rayless environment, that the Face of Jesus shines. It shines with an unborrowed glory, a glory all its own. Nothing assists it; everything resists it; but it shines, and we see it and are glad.

There was an old belief that in its hour of death the swan *sang*. In His moment of death *Jesus* uttered a strain of triumph. When the great darkness had lasted three hours, the radiance in the soul of Jesus found expression, and He cried with a loud voice: 'It is finished; Father, into Thy hands I commend my spirit!' With that song on His lips, He died. It was not the moment when men expected Him to die. They were surprised. The mere physical cross did not account for it. It can only be accounted for by the supposition that some great emotion had ruptured His heart. But what was that emotion? It was not despair. It was not the sense of being forsaken by His Father.

It was not the rupture which we popularly call a broken heart. When we speak of a broken heart we mean a heart broken by grief. But, if it were good English, it would be perfectly good physiology to speak of a heart broken by *joy*. No doubt the physical heart of Jesus had been weakened by a long train of burdens, and there was wanted only one final strain to snap its cords asunder. But that final strain was to come not from the flesh but from the spirit—not from a burden of care but from a weight of glory. The last chord of the harp was snapped by a stroke of ecstasy; it was a rupture through rapture!

And what was the cause of that gleam which shot across the dying hour of Jesus? It was the sense of a completed development, 'It is finished!' Remember, no claimant for the office of Messiah could prove his claim till he had reached the setting sun; it was only at evening time there could be perfect light. The required surrender to the Father must be from dawn to dark. It was not enough that the claimant should go up to Mount Moriah 'early

in the morning'; the morning sacrifice must
be endorsed by the noon, the midday, and
the twilight; only in the *last rays* of twilight
could the aspirant say, 'It is finished!' None
had ever reached that terminus before. They
had all fainted; they had all grown weary.
Many had made high resolves in the dawn;
none had sustained them through the day.
Some had sunk at morning; some had
withered at midday; some had fainted in
the afternoon. But now, at last, there befell
a wonder. One human soul *arrived at the
evening* of the sacrificial day! He arrived
alone; He was the first to discover the new
country—the reconciled heart of the Father.
Yet, solitary as He was, He knew that He was
the pioneer of millions. He was footsore, but
His foot was on the land. There was no
possibility of any more sea. He had reached
the furthest limit of the path of sacrifice. He
had realised the dream of the temple; He had
realised the dream on the banks of Jordan.
He had kept till evening the promise He had
made to the blood-red morning sun. He had

finished that work of love which in the days of childhood He had projected for His Father.

LET me bring Thee a wreath, O Jesus! Let me bring it now and here—to the spot which the world calls Thy grave! There are many wreaths of *pity* on that spot; but it is not a wreath of pity that *I* would like to bring. Not a cypress, but a laurel, would I lay on the steps of Calvary. Often have I looked at my brother's grave and said, 'How unfinished is the work of life!' But when I gaze on *Thy* tomb I have the opposite feeling; I say, '*This* Life was rounded, perfected!' They tell me that the path of glory leads but to the grave; but *Thy* path to the grave led to glory. There is a *garden* in the place where they laid Thee; it will always be there. When I see Thy dying, the beauty will ever predominate over the gloom. Therefore I will bring no cypress to Thy cross. Tears are out of place there; pity is unseemly there; worship alone can reign there. Thy crown glitters in the dust; Thy Face shines in the gloom; Thy kingdom comes in the cloud; Thy sceptre waves in the pierced hand. Thou art powerful in Thy prostration; Thou hast dominion in Thy dying; Thou art conqueror in Thy final cry. The wreath I bring to Calvary shall be a wreath of glory!

CHAPTER XXIII

THE MEANING OF EASTER MORNING

I HAVE now completed the attempt which was the purpose of these volumes. I have tried to trace the process as delineated by the Gospel narrative, whereby Incarnate Love sought by a lifelong surrender to compensate the Father for a world's lovelessness. The last hour of that lifelong surrender opened and closed in Calvary. The words 'It is finished!' mark in the soul of Jesus the sense of a completed process. He has yielded up His will to the Father from dawn to dark. That expiatory offering of His soul which was begun in the morning has been continued without intermission, and perfected at eventide.

I have no right to prolong this book beyond what the Gospel narrative declares to be the last note of biographical development. I know

there are many scenes of the Life which still
remain; but they are not scenes of development. I do not say that some day I may not
write a book on the Portrait of the Resurrection
Christ; it is a subject of great interest and of
profound importance. But should I do so, it
will not be a third volume of the present work,
but a new work. The expiatory sacrifice of
Jesus was finished on Calvary. Easter Morning
added nothing to its completeness. So far as
the surrender of Jesus is concerned, Calvary is
a climax; greater love hath no man than this!
The surrender of will, conceived in the aspirations of childhood, begun in the temptations
of the wilderness, deepened in the sympathy
with man, tested by the threatened failure of
His fondest dreams, is crowned and culminated
by His words on the cross, 'Father, into Thy
hands I commend my spirit!'

Here, then, is the fitting place to pause.
There can be no grander spot in which to drop
the curtain. It is a spot not of defeat but of
glory. The Form on which our eye gazes is a
conqueror's form. It is the figure of One who

has seen the travail of his own soul, and is satisfied with the retrospect, who has vanquished His last peril, and need fear no more. The development of the work of Jesus is complete on Calvary. But it remains for us to ask two questions bearing on the relation of the Old Picture to the New. We will take the one in the present, and the other in the following chapter.

And first. Why do the scenes in the *great gallery* not pause at Calvary? If the development of Jesus is complete, why extend the picture? Why is it that when next we stand as artistic spectators we stand before a new scene? Why is it that, two days after that preternatural darkness, the Portrait of Jesus glitters in the sun? Surely in the mind of the artist there must have lurked a sense that the original Picture was, after all, incomplete— after all, unfinished!

And the mind of the artist judged rightly. I, too, hold that the Cross of Calvary leaves a want unsupplied; all I say is that the want did not lie in the *development of Jesus.* On

Calvary the work of Jesus is complete, finished, perfect in all its parts; but there is still something wanting to the *Picture*. What is that desideratum? What is that missing link which the narrative of the Resurrection supplies? That is the question which now presses upon us, and it is a question of deep interest. 'The power of Christ's Resurrection,' has become a proverbial phrase. The man who first uttered it stood very near the Portrait; he occupied the front seat in the gallery; he had a perfect view. I should like to know what to this man, Paul, was the secret of the power he speaks of. I think I should be disposed to take his word for it, since he gazed from a distance so near. I am not speaking of him as a witness to the *fact*; that is a question for the apologists. But I should like to know wherein to Paul lay the *power* of Christ's resurrection. And this I *can* know, for he has told me. Let us consider his testimony.

Now, in looking into the mind of Paul, we find something which at first sight surprises us. We should have expected that the value to him of the Resurrection Portrait would have been its revelation of Christ's greatness. Strange to say, that is not his view. The revelation of Christ's greatness is to him a thing already accomplished and needing no proof from Easter Morning. Nay, Paul is not afraid to invert the order. So far from regarding Christ's resurrection as a proof of His greatness, he regards our sense of His greatness as a proof of His resurrection. In that remarkable passage of 1 Cor. xv., in which he defends the gospel of Easter Day, he says that if the immortality of man be untrue, there would follow five impossible consequences. The first and foremost of these is the striking statement, 'If there be no resurrection of the dead, then is *Christ* not risen.' In other words, what he says is this: 'If the soul be not immortal, there will follow the impossible consequence that Christ is dead—that the life in whom our aspiration reposes has become a thing, a clod of the valley. Deny immortality, and you commit the mental contradiction of denying the eternity of Jesus. Are you able to associate Jesus with death! Is it not to you a contradiction in terms! Is not the very statement "Christ is dead" the putting together of two incongruous things—the union of perfect life and blank nothingness! When one says "Christ is dead," you instinctively cry, "Impossible! if *He* be dead, then death cannot mean what *I* call dying."'

Paul, then, does not regard the resurrection of Jesus in the light of a personal reward miraculously enhancing His glory. He looks upon it as the inevitable result of a glory already existing. It was not an immortality *conferred*; it was an immortality emerging. He says elsewhere in so many words that the immortal life of Jesus was the life He bore about in His dying body. He was not immortal because He rose; He rose because He was immortal. The Resurrection was not a root but a flower. The root lay in the Christ of Calvary—the Christ who could suffer and still be strong. The secret of His immortality was not the rolling away of the sepulchral stone; it was the holiness that sustained the

wilderness and the cross. Easter was not a
miraculous intervention on behalf of Jesus;
the miracle would have been His continuing
under the power of *death*. Had there been no
resurrection, Christ would have been dead—
there would have been a violation of spiritual
law. The rolling away of the stone *prevented*
a miracle; it restored the order of nature; it
re-established the harmony between life and
its environment.

One of the dearest disciples and closest
companions of Paul has given direct expression to the idea that the Resurrection was no
miracle. I allude to the earliest of ecclesiastical
historians—the writer of the Acts. Speaking
of the rising of Jesus, he uses the remarkable
words: 'Having loosed the pains of death,
because it was not possible that He should be
holden of it.' What he really means to say is
that to accomplish the rising of the Son of
Man no new force had to be added to those
already existing. It was not required that
Jesus should be made immortal. Jesus was
already immortal. Even at His hour of death

there was an *incongruity* between Him and death. His death was a miracle; it was quite impossible that it should be a *perpetuated* miracle. Something must intervene to restore the broken balance of nature. Jesus had in Him the root of immortality—something which made it inconceivable that His flesh should see corruption. That thing was holiness. His purity of heart demanded that He should see *God*, and *not* corruption. The secret of His immortality was in Himself, not in His resurrection. He loosed the pains of death because He was Himself stronger than death. That strength is our hope of glory. Easter is merely a manifestation of that strength—an effect of it, a result of it. Christ is, in the deepest sense, the cause of His own rising; in Christ, and not in His rising, lies our vision of immortality.

According, then, to the earliest view of the subject, the value of Easter Morning does not lie in wreathing Jesus with the crown of immortality. It does *not* so wreath Him; He was wreathed with that crown long before. I may remark in passing that my individual

impression has always coincided with this early
view. Believing, as I do, in the manifestation
of Jesus after death, I believe it on other
grounds than the revealing of His immortality.
To me His immortality needs no such revelation. As I stand in the great gallery and read
the Face of Jesus, as I mark the expressions
of that Face through all the scenes from
Galilee to Calvary, I feel that He is already
immortal. I feel, so far as my sense of His
immortality is concerned, that I need no testimony from the open grave. It would not
disconcert me, on this point, if a new and
earlier Bible were found which closed its record
at the Cross of Calvary. I should still feel
that in this Portrait of the Son of Man I had
the highest possible evidence of the existence
of a soul invulnerable by death. I am impressed that here is a Life which is going to
His Father, which is bound for heaven, which
has already obtained a key to open the golden
gate. I feel that *this* soul, at least, is the
accepted of the Lord—that, whatever be the
state of others, this Man, at all events, has

passed the flaming sword of the Cherubim and planted His feet in the Paradise of God.

I agree, then, with Paul and with the early Church generally, that the opening of the grave was no addition to the majesty of Jesus. The value of the open sepulchre to Jesus does not lie in any increase of His personal glory. Where, then, does it lie; what is the meaning of Easter Morning? Let us stand again in the gallery beside the man in front of the Picture; let us once more ask Paul. He has had his eye on both the night and the morning aspect of the Portrait. He has studied it amid the shadows; he has studied it in the roseate hours. He has brought to the study a combination of faculties unequalled among his contemporaries. He has been on both sides of the Christian controversy; he has been on many sides of Christian experience. He has been a man of large nature. He has been a Roman to the Romans, a Greek to the Corinthians, a Celt to the Galatians. His opinion will be worth having, and it will be an impartial opinion; let us ask Paul.

And, indeed, when we get the answer we are struck with its impartiality. Paul had never seen the earthly Jesus; he had been disparaged because he had never seen Him. He had every temptation to undervalue the expiating work of Galilee and Jerusalem, every temptation to exalt a new and mystical Christ on the Resurrection Heights of Olivet. Does he yield to that temptation? On the contrary, he says that the glory of Easter Morning is simply that it *endorsed* that expiating work which with his outward eyes he had never seen. He describes the value of Christ's resurrection in the memorable words, 'He was raised for our justification.'

What does he mean by that? What do *you* mean by using a similar expression in common life? When do you say, 'You see I have been justified in what I did'? It is when something has happened which proves you to have been right. Now, that is precisely what Paul means. He says: 'You have taken this man for your Messiah—your sin-bearer. You have accepted him as the Mediator between you and your

Father. There were many things that seemed to mock your choice. He was despised and rejected of men, a man of sorrows and acquainted with grief. He seemed to tread a path of silence, a path of obscurity, a path the reverse of that prescribed for your national Messiah. But here at last there has come the Father's audible "Amen"! Here at last you are proved to have been right! Your choice has been justified. There has come a flash from the sky, a voice from the silence. The curtain of death has been rent into fragments, and you have been allowed to see what is already known in *heaven* — that this finished Life is accepted as the Expiation for human sin.'

With Paul, then, I regard Easter Morning as the Father's audible 'Amen' to the work of Jesus. It was the only audible 'Amen' which had yet been uttered. Amid all the wonders of the Galilean and Jerusalem ministries there had been one desideratum ; there had been no voice from the Father to the *world*. There had been voices to *Jesus*—intimations that with

His personal life the Father was well pleased;
but there had been no voice addressed to the
ear of the world. Gethsemane's message had,
indeed, been one of good tidings for man; but
it had been spoken in the ear of Jesus alone,
and life had been too short to enable Him to
reveal it. What more fitting than that it
should be revealed after life had closed! Easter
Morning sent a sunbeam of heaven over every
inch of that gallery which held the Portrait of
Jesus. To all the admirers of that Portrait it
breathed a voice of welcome, admitting them
as students of the Great Academy. That is
the meaning, that is the glory, of Easter
Morning. It is the one voice that says to the
world, 'Through this Beloved Son the Father
is pleased with you.' Why is it that we centre
in the resurrection of Christ rather than in
the resurrection of *Lazarus*? The latter was
equally an exhibition of power, and it could
have been corroborated by a larger multitude;
why does *Christ's* rising bear the glory? It is
because the resurrection of Christ is what the
resurrection of Lazarus does not profess to

be—a message of reconciliation. It is because what we seek from any Easter Morning is not a mere declaration that we are immortal, but a declaration that we are immortal *children of God*. We want to know, not merely that we are freed from death, but that we are accepted 'in the Beloved.' Lazarus perpetuated in his grave-clothes would, after all, be a sorry gain. The bells of Bethany may ring the message, 'Live for ever!' but the bells of Easter Morning ring a message nobler still, 'All hail!'

BEHOLD us in Christ, O Father; accept us in Thy Beloved! See in Him the finished picture of ourselves! Thou hast been working as the artist works—striving to perfect each portrait of each human soul. In all the gallery there is only one that has responded to Thy touch — only one that is altogether lovely. But that One has shown the possibility for all. Behold us in Him! See in Him what we *might* be! When our humanity reveals its blemishes, when Thou art tempted to turn Thine eyes from us in artistic despair, let this one Face shine before Thee! Let His beauty be Thy hope for *me*! Let His purity be Thy dream of me! Let His sacrifice be Thy prophecy of me! Behold in Him the possibilities of Thy Spirit in Man! He is the *first* rose of our summer, and as yet He is all alone. But when Thou gazest on Him Thou seest in Thy *heart* the roses which are not yet in Thy *garden*. *Keep* my roses in Thy heart, O Lord; let them bloom already *there*! Ere ever they are rooted and grounded in the soil, ere ever they have opened their petals to the day, ere ever they are warmed by the sunshine or watered by the rain, look upon my roses as risen with Jesus! Create within Thy thought each plant before it grows; and let the light which nourishes Thine ideal garden be the beauty of the Son of Man!

CHAPTER XXIV

HAS THE CROWN SUPERSEDED THE CROSS?

THE question I have made the title of this chapter is the second of those which I proposed to ask. Put in other words, it amounts to this: 'Is the Face of Jesus which appeared after death the same Face which through these pages we have studied in the great gallery?' If it is not, we should experience a thrill of regret. We should do so even if it were proved that the Resurrection Face of Jesus was less marred than the Original Countenance. Probably, in all circumstances, *love* would feel this. If the offer were made to you to have the face of some dear friend transformed into the more glorious countenance of an angel, you would certainly cry, 'No; I would rather have it as it is—blemishes and all!' But the feeling would be much stronger in the case of the marred Visage of *Jesus*, for the marredness of that Visage is to the Christian a part of its beauty. To take away *that* from the gallery would be to paint Christ with Calvary left out ; and the omission would be resented in the interest both of art and religion. We hear a great deal about the *exaltation* of Jesus—about the crown of thorns being exchanged for a crown of glory. I greatly prefer the paradox of the Fourth Gospel: 'Your *sorrow* shall be turned into joy.' What we want to see in Jesus is not an exchange but an efflorescence. We want to see Him glorified, not by His exaltation *above* the cross, but by His exaltation *on* the cross. We want to see, in short, the glorifying of Christ's *sorrow* ; and we shall not be satisfied with any sequel which simply lifts the Son of Man out of His troubles.

Accordingly, we shall look with some interest for the answer to the question, 'What does the Resurrection narrative propose to do with that Portrait of Jesus with which we have become familiar and which we have learned to love?'

Now, there is a point to which I wish to direct attention because it seems to me of great importance in determining this question. Has it ever struck you that the Resurrection narrative is, in the scenes through which it passes, essentially retrospective? If you will only grant —what a large number of critics believe—that the fishing expedition of John xxi. has been recorded in the wrong place, you will be able to come to a remarkable conclusion. You will find that the Resurrection Life of Jesus is a repetition, on the upper road and with panoramic swiftness, of the nature and order of those scenes which constitute the features of His earlier ministries.

Let us recall the order of these earlier ministries. Jesus begins in simple Galilee. His first experience is an experience not of communities but of individuals. He meets men as they are—goes to their marriage feasts, joins in their daily avocations. But when He has attracted them He begins to combine them. He passes from the position of an individual teacher to the position of a corporate head. He forms a league of pity. It has but twelve men; but it is the nucleus of a coming kingdom. By and by the nucleus expands; the twelve become the five thousand; the cup passes from the hand of the disciples to the hand of the multitude. As His circle widens, His message enlarges. He speaks at first on the lines of the past—expanding what the prophets had taught, deepening what had been said by 'the men of old time.' But by and by He takes a higher flight. He ceases to be merely an interpreter of the *past*. He claims to have a *new* commandment, to breathe a fresh spirit into humanity, to impart to the world an additional stream of life.

Now, look at the comparison between this order of events and the order of events described in the combined accounts of Christ's Resurrection ministry; I have been greatly struck with its similarity—I had nearly said, its identity—of sequence. Here *too* we have a Christ who begins in Galilee. Here *too* His first manifestations are to private individuals— are dictated by the personal leanings of His heart. He appears to Mary Magdalene; He appears to the other Mary; He appears to Peter. He meets His fishermen disciples, as He had done of yore, in the midst of their daily toil; He stands by the lake of Tiberias and bids them cast their nets once more. Then comes a transition like that we meet in the early Gospel' story. Jesus appears to the Twelve *collectively*. Hitherto He has met only *individuals* in His Resurrection form; He now manifests Himself to the united league of pity. And for the *second* time we have an ordination sermon on a mountain of Galilee—a sermon which ordains these primitive missionaries to teach throughout all nations those practical precepts which in the days of His first ministry had been uttered, perhaps, on that very hill.

By and by we have another stage in the Resurrection Life of Jesus; and *again* it repeats the sequence of the primitive ministry. In that ministry we saw the twelve widen into the five thousand; the cup of communion was committed to the hands of the multitude.

And the enlargement of the league is repeated here. 'Afterward,' cries Paul, speaking of the Resurrection Christ, 'He was seen of above five hundred brethren at once.' After the twelve came the five hundred; after the disciples came the multitude. The rhythm of the Resurrection has followed the rhythm of the Incarnation. In both there has been a progress from the inner to the outer circle. In both there has been an advance from the individual to the masses. In both there has been an expansion from the sphere of domestic interest into the sphere of public interest. In both there has been an extension of the field of missionary labour from the limits of a native locality to the needs of man as man.

There is even a strong similarity between the geographical transitions of these ministries. Both began with Galilee; both ended by shifting their final scene from Galilee to Jerusalem. And in both the change of scene is accompanied by a change of teaching. The Resurrection Christ who stands among the hills of Galilee teaches the same homely lessons

which in Galilee He taught before. And when
the Resurrection Christ comes to Jerusalem,
He adopts those other lessons which in *Jerusalem* He taught before. He no longer gives
utterance to the aphorisms of the daily life.
He lifts men *beyond* the day, beyond the world
—into a house not made with hands, eternal in
the heavens. He breathes upon them a higher
air. He points them to a life not seen by earthly
eye, not heard by earthly ear, not cognis-
able by earthly sense. He repeats the offer
of that mysterious peace which comes through
shut doors — which manifests itself where
nothing can account for it. Above all, He
repeats the scene in the upper room ; He is
known to His disciples in the breaking of
bread. It is a fuller communion than that
before His death. In the communion before
Calvary death was only a prospect to Him ;
in the communion after Resurrection death
was a retrospect ; He could give the experience of a completed life.

Such is the parallel which has suggested
itself to me between the ministry of the

Resurrection Christ and the ministry of that
Christ whose Portrait we have been considering. I have dwelt upon it, not to emphasise
a curious speculation, but to support a very
sober view. If this parallel be well founded,
it will follow that the Crown is not meant to
supersede the Cross—that the glory of the
Resurrection is its removal of obstacles *in the
path of* the Cross. But, waiving this parallel
between the manifestations of the Risen Christ
and the events of the antecedent ministry, let
us look at the former by themselves and on
their own account. When I survey these
manifestations of the Risen Christ there is one
thing which impresses me beyond all others,
and that is the *sacrificial* character of the
narratives. I think they are more sacrificial
than those of the previous ministries. In
the previous ministries nearly all the acts of
sacrifice are done by *Jesus*. But in this Resurrection ministry the sacrifice is shared by the
disciple; the servant has taken up the cross
of his Lord. I am deeply struck with this.
It is not a peculiarity of any one incident; it

runs like a thread of gold through all the series. A moment's gaze at the Resurrection Portrait of Jesus will make this clear.

The very opening incident suggests sacrifice. Magdalene has found her Lord, alive. She is in rapturous joy. She assumes He is come to remain. She clings to Him with a wild tenacity —a tenacity which says in effect, 'I will never again let you go!' He answers: 'Ah, but you must! It is vain for you thus to hold me. Cling to me not, for I am not yet ascended to my Father—not yet in the possession of my perfect joy. Let it be a comfort to you to know that *your bereavement* is the *world's gain*; I can do greater things for men when I am in the presence of my Father. Meantime, it may help you to bear this bereavement if you re-member that your brethren *also* are bereaved. Go and tell those who have *not* seen me that for a moment *you have* seen me. There are some who may never get even the temporary glimpse *you* have had. Tell these that I am not dead, that you have seen me alive, that I have ascended to my Father.' And Magdalene departs-to obey the command; she carries the burden of humanity in the Easter Dawn.

Again. Three forms are seen treading the road to Emmaus. Two of them are those of Christian disciples; the third is the figure of the Risen Jesus. The disciples do not know Jesus; but, without knowing Him, they are thrilled by His utterance. They complain of the failure of the hopes they had formed of Him. Jesus still keeps His incognito. Instead of dispelling their fears by a direct revelation of Himself, He appeals to their reason and their heart. He strives to make them see His beauty, not as the result of resurrection, but as the result of sacrifice. Speaking under the disguise of a stranger, He says, '*Ought* not Christ to have suffered these things in order to enter into His glory?'

And the words seem to have had a good effect. There follows a fine act of unselfishness on the part of these disciples. When they reach the door of their own house they say to the stranger, 'Abide with us, for it is toward evening, and the day is far spent.'

Sermon-writers and hymn-writers have lost the
point of this narrative. They persist in regarding the request as the cry of helpless souls
beseeching Jesus to be near them. They
forget that these men did not know to whom
they were speaking, that they took Jesus for
a stranger. When they said, ' It is toward
evening, and the day is far spent,' they did not
mean, ' *We* shall find it very dark,' but, '*You*
will find it very dark.' It was an act of pure
humanitarianism—done actually for Christ,
but believed to be done for another. It was
a cup of cold water given to Jesus ' only in
the name of a disciple.' The whole scene was
an unconscious yet visible representation
of the words, ' Inasmuch as ye did it unto
one of the least of these my brethren, ye have
done it unto me.'

They enter the house ; they sit down to
partake of the nightly meal. But the presence
of Jesus makes the ordinary meal what He
wished it to be—a sacrament—that one Sacrament which commemorates His Sacrifice. And
here, strange to say, the incognito is lifted ;

He is recognised 'in the breaking of bread'. There are those who after long years have been identified by an attitude. But it is strange, from an artistic point of view, that the Christ of Easter Day should have been identified by an attitude bearing the reminiscence of *Calvary*. One would have thought that the recognition would have fastened on something more majestic—that the Resurrection Form would have reminded these disciples of the afterglow of that glory which had illumined Him on the Transfiguration Mount. But no; it is not the Mount but the upper room that is the medium of recognition. It comes from an attitude reminding, not of His glory, but of His humiliation. What they recognise is the Broken Body—the Body broken for *them*. The recognition of the Christ who had passed into a life beyond the grave is effected mainly by the memory of sacrificial love.

With striking consistency is the idea maintained in the episode of *Thomas*. Thomas recognises his Lord by the print of the nails. The presence of such a feature in the Resurrection Body of Jesus is artistically startling. To admit a memorial of pain into a picture of the heavenly state was a bold thing. It would have been bold in any age; it was specially bold in *that* age. It was an age that reverenced the strong, that reverenced the beautiful. It was a period when a physical blemish was deemed a disgrace, when Divine power meant bodily power. To such a world the spectacle presented by the gallery on Easter Morning must have been as new as it was appalling —a Form that has risen to the sphere of the immortals is seen bearing the mark of its earthly wounds! It is the inauguration of a new ideal of heaven, nay, of a new ideal of God—an ideal in which power will be proportionate to suffering, in which the ability to succour pain will be commensurate with the capacity to feel it.

And what else than this is the meaning of these words of Jesus on the mountain of Galilee, 'All power is given unto me in heaven and on earth; go ye, therefore, and teach all nations'? The power of which

Jesus speaks is sympathetic power; otherwise
there would be no meaning in the word
'therefore.' He says, ' I have received the
power of universal sympathy; go, therefore,
and help universal Man!' And *where* has He
received it? On the *heavenly* side of death?
No, on the earthly side. He has received
His culminating power, not from resurrection,
but from death itself. His last stage of
development was in the depths of the valley;
there He met man as man. The flower
which Jesus wears on Easter Morning is not
the flower of Eden but the flower of Gethsemane. Eden could *never* unite 'all nations';
but Gethsemane can; there is not a common
joy, but there *is* a common sorrow. Therefore
it is His *death* that makes Him our King! It is
His *cross* that we lift! It is His *sorrow* that
we elevate! It is His *pain* that we glorify!
It is His *sacrifice* that we perpetuate! Paul
speaks of men being caught up to meet the
Risen Christ—the Christ 'in the air.' But it is
not the elevation that attracts them; it is the
object elevated. They are drawn to the height

because the *valley* is mirrored there; they are tempted to the sunbeam because it holds the *shadow* in its bosom. The glory of Easter Morning is the sacrificial red upon its sky.

I THANK Thee, O Lord, for this new ideal of heaven! The veil of the temple has *indeed* been rent in twain! I had altogether different ideas of the life beyond death—the Resurrection Life. I thought heaven was a place where there was no trace of the nail-prints, no room for sacrificial love. I thank Thee that Thou hast rent the veil and hast let me see through! I praise Thee, O Lord, for that vision! I was afraid my love would die from disuse, die from having nothing to do. I bless Thee that Thy Risen Form has gone down into Galilee—down to those who sit in the valley of the shadow! I bless Thee that Thy heavenly life is a life of ministration—that *still* Thou art known in the breaking of bread! I bless Thee that under the folds of the bright garment Thou keepest the print of the nails—

the memory of human tears! Be *mine* Thy heaven, Thou Christ of Easter Day! Be mine beyond the grave that ministrant life of Thine! Be mine Thy home of helpfulness, Thy Paradise of pity! Let my happy land of Beulah be a land of successful burden-bearing —a land which gives facilities for wiping all tears from all eyes! Then shall my hope of heaven make me pure on earth; then shall my sight of coming glory prepare me for the ministry to present pain. I shall learn the lesson of love's eternity when the light of Easter Morning tells me that Thy first hour in Paradise was an hour in Galilee!

Printed by T. and A. CONSTABLE, Printers to Her Majesty
at the Edinburgh University Press

Lightning Source UK Ltd.
Milton Keynes UK
UKHW030954031218
333380UK00009B/427/P